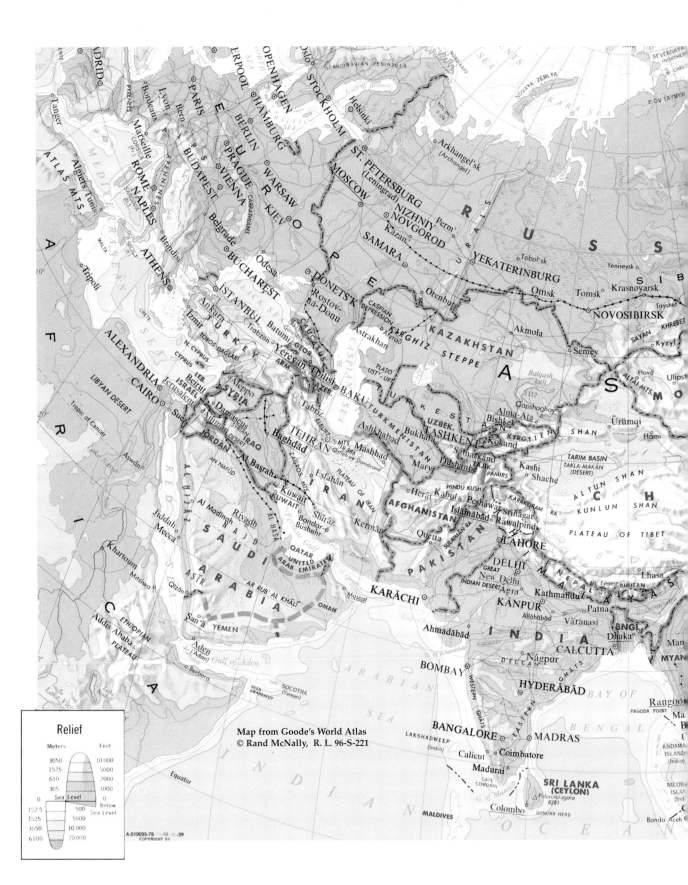

Map from Goode's World Atlas
© Rand McNally, R. L. 96-S-221

Relief

Meters		Feet
3050		10 000
1525		5000
610		2000
305		1000
0	Sea Level	0
		Below
		Sea Level
1525		500
1525		5000
3050		10 000
6100		20 000

A-519695-76 11-19 12 -39
COPYRIGHT BY

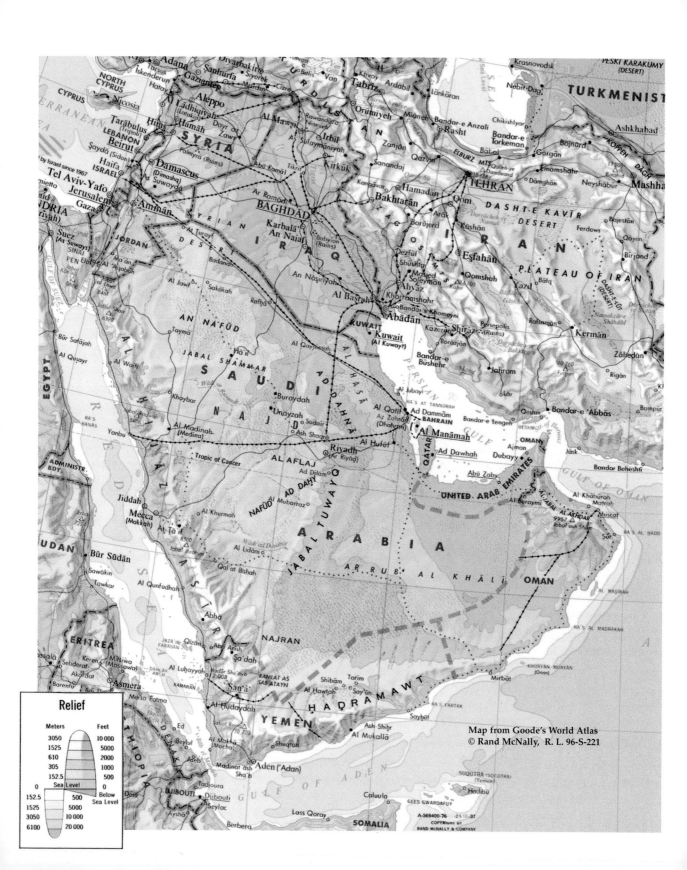

Map from Goode's World Atlas
© Rand McNally, R. L. 96-S-221

Relief

Meters		Feet
3050		10 000
1525		5000
610		2000
305		1000
152.5		500
0	Sea Level	0
		Below
152.5	500	Sea Level
1525	5000	
3050	10 000	
6100	20 000	

A-569400-76   21-18-37

COPYRIGHT BY
RAND McNALLY & COMPANY

Enchantment of the World

QATAR

by Byron Augustin and Rebecca A. Augustin

Consultant for Qatar: John Duke Anthony, Ph.D., President and Chief
Executive Officer, National Council on U.S.-Arab Relations, Washington, D.C.

CHILDREN'S PRESS®
A Division of Grolier Publishing
New York • London • Hong Kong • Sydney
Danbury, Connecticut

The spice shop in the old souq, *or market, is a reminder of old Qatar.*

Project Editor and Design: Jean Blashfield Black

Library of Congress
Cataloging-in-Publication Data

Augustin, Byron.
   Qatar / by Byron and Rebecca Augustin.
      p. cm. -- (Enchantment of the world)
   Includes index.
Summary: Describes the geography, history, culture, economy, and people of the small Middle Eastern country of Qatar.
   ISBN 0-516-20303-7
   1. Qatar--Juvenile literature. [1. Qatar.] I. Augustin, Rebecca. II. Title. III. Series.
DS247.Q3A94   1996
953.63--dc21   96-49593
                                                      CIP
                                                      AC

Photo credits ©: AFP/Corbis-Bettman: 46; Art Resource: 25 (Giraudon); Byron Augustin: cover, 4, 6 bottom, 8, 9, 10, 11, 12, 13, 17, 19, 22, 26, 27, 28, 33 right, 34, 37 top, 38, 39, 41,, 45, 51, 54, 64, 67, 69, 72, 73, 75, 76, 78 left, 79 top, 81 bottom right, 81 top, 84 left, 87, 88, 93, 96 top, 96 inset right, 97, 98, 99 right, 101 left, 102 top, 103 inset, 104 top, 104 bottom, 106, 108, 109; Corbis-Bettman: 20, 29; Ministry of Information & Culture: 42 left and right, 79 bottom; North Wind Picture Archives: 24, 30; Rebecca Augustin: 15 bottom right, 16, 31, 37 bottom, 49 right, 50, 52, 56, 59, 61, 77, 78 right, 81 bottom left, 82, 85, 89, 91 top left, 91 top right, 92 left, 94 top, 99 left, 102 inset, 103 bottom; UPI/Corbis/Betmann: 33 left, 100, 110; Valan Photos: 6 top (Paul J. Janosi), 23, 36, 91 bottom, 94 inset, 96 bottom, 101 right (Joyce Photographics), 5, 14, 15 top, 18, 21, 49 left, 55, 60, 63, 65, 70, 81 center left, 84 bottom, 84 top right, 92 right (Christine Osborne), 15 bottom left (R. Werburton).

Cover photo: Coffee pot sculpture and the Sheraton Hotel, Doha

Modern Qataris are just as fascinated by computers as the rest of the world.

TABLE OF CONTENTS

The two main facts of life in Qatar are the sea (above) and the desert (below), with its scarcity of water and vegetation.

Chapter 1

A DESERT PENINSULA

Qatar is one of those faraway places with a strange-sounding name, which is pronounced KAHT-uhr. Frequently an answer in crossword puzzles, Qatar was not well-known outside of the Arab world until recent years. Now, more people are learning about this small, enchanting country.

Located along the western coast of the Persian Gulf, which is also called the Arabian Gulf, Qatar protrudes like a thumb from the eastern shore of the Arabian Peninsula. It stretches northeast almost 100 miles (160 kilometers), but it is little more than 50 miles (80 kilometers) across, at its widest point. Slightly smaller than the state of Connecticut, Qatar has a total land area of 4,247 square miles (11,437 square kilometers).

Surrounded by a coastline of more than 350 miles (563 kilometers) and many small islands, the citizens of Qatar have traditionally focused on the sea. The little nation's only land boundary is less than 32 miles (50 kilometers) in length, where southern Qatar touches Saudi Arabia and the United Arab Emirates. The exact land boundary has been in dispute for many years.

LANDFORMS

A peninsula composed mostly of sandstone and limestone, Qatar has risen only slightly from the waters of what was once a

Most of Qatar is surrounded by the blue waters of the Persian, or Arabian, Gulf. It has very little natural fresh water, but since the discovery of petroleum resources, the Qataris have been able to desalinate, or remove the salt from, the plentiful seawater for such uses as filling this hotel swimming pool.

larger sea. For the most part, its surface is flat with little change in elevation. This flat surface is covered with sand, gravel, and cobblestones. Vegetation is sparse if not totally absent.

There is a gradual increase in elevation from the east to the west coast. The highest point on the peninsula is found in a small range of hills, known as the Jebel Dukhan, which reach a height of almost 250 feet (75 meters) above sea level. The range runs north to south for about 35 miles (55 kilometers) and parallels the west coast. It is little more than 5 miles (8 kilometers) across at its widest point. However, because Qatar is so flat, on a clear day, vast distances can be viewed from the top of the ridge. Qatar's

The sand dunes along the bay at Khor al-Udaid in southeastern Qatar
make a spectacular place to explore with a four-wheel-drive vehicle.

major oil field lies beneath the low hills of Jebel Dukhan.

In the southeastern corner of the country, graceful sand dunes sweep down to the very edge of the waters of the Persian Gulf. Located along the shore of a protected bay known as Khor al-Udaid, this site is a favorite tourist destination for Qatari citizens. The impressive dunes, which reach heights of 130 feet (40 meters), swirl in regularly changing patterns as the wind shapes a fascinating landscape. Tourists arrive in the early morning to observe the sun as it rises across the gulf waters, casting a soft light onto the dunes. The bay is also a popular site to view wildlife. During their annual migrations, thousands of birds drop down to feed in the shallow waters of the bay.

In the north-central part of the country, there are many depressions in the surface of the land that collect rainwater during the winter months. These drainage basins, known as al-Riyadh (the "gardens"), are rapidly becoming the most important area of

Sheep and some other livestock can survive on the scant vegetation that grows in the sand after a slight rain.

cultivated agriculture in Qatar. The soil is fertile and an underground aquifer, or deposit of water, provides fresh water for irrigation of vegetables, fruits, and other specialty crops.

ISLANDS

Several islands located offshore are claimed as part of Qatar's national territory. Ra's Rakan is off the northern tip of the peninsula. Qarradh and Umm Tais are to the west. Shra'ouh is found southeast of the industrial town of Umm Said and is noted as a stop for migrating birds. In recent years, the islands of Halul, Sifliyya, and Hawar Archipelago have become better known.

Sifliyya Island, which is situated only 3.5 miles (6 kilometers) north of the capital of Doha, has become a major tourist site with

10

Not all the surface of Qatar is sand. These limestone deposits have been carved out by rains over many years, until finally the roof of the cave collapsed, creating a cavity called a cenote. The bottom of the cenote reaches down into underground water.

its long sandy beaches. Halul Island, about 60 miles (96 kilometers) northeast of Doha, has developed into a major oil-storage center and port for shipping Qatar's oil and gas resources.

The Hawar Archipelago is a chain of islands found between Qatar and the tiny island nation of Bahrain. Some islands of the archipelago are less than 1.5 miles (2.5 kilometers) from Qatar but almost 15 miles (24 kilometers) from Bahrain. However, Bahrain was recognized by the British in 1939 as having political jurisdiction over the Hawar Islands. The government of Qatar believes that Bahrain's claim is invalid and has asked the International Court of Justice to rule in its favor. The question is before the court.

The brief winter rains may be enough to cause a normally dry creek bed to fill with rushing water.

CLIMATE

Qatar is one of the world's true desert nations. Rainfall is extremely rare and most of the country receives less than 2 inches (5 centimeters) of precipitation during the year. December is the wettest month, and the winter season accounts for most of the precipitation. In the summer, there may be periods when no rain falls for forty to fifty consecutive days. Although little rain falls during the year, the relative humidity is quite high (80 to 90 percent) along the coast of the Persian Gulf. The humidity drops substantially away from the sea. The summers are very hot with daytime temperatures reaching 110° to 115° F. (43° to 46°C) regularly. These extreme temperatures cause people to perspire freely, so they must consume lots of liquids to prevent dehydration. It is also important for them to wear loose-fitting clothing that

These palm trees are growing in a low-lying depression where the scarce winter rainfall may collect, giving the place the temporary but misleading appearance of an oasis.

allows air to circulate around the body. Garments made of cotton are normally worn in the summer because they absorb moisture.

Temperatures during the winter months are pleasant, with an average of 60° F. (15° C). Winter nights can actually be quite cool, with the temperature dipping into the low 40s (about 5°C). Qatari citizens enjoy the winters, but they frequently vacation during summer in countries with cooler climates to escape the oppressive heat.

Winds blow across the peninsula on a regular basis. The winds that blow from the north, known as the *shamal,* may be very unpleasant. They absorb what little moisture is available and carry sand and dust high into the air. Dust storms and sandstorms are

*Qatar's soil and climate do not allow the growing of plants to feed
people without a great deal of special cultivation and irrigation
carried out in limited locations.*

common in the interior and on many days, a dusty haze covers the
entire country, limiting visibility.

PLANTS AND ANIMALS

Many people believe that the deserts are totally void of
vegetation and composed only of shifting sand dunes. In reality,
this is seldom true. While vegetation may be sparse, many unique
plants have adapted to survive in the desert. In Qatar, more than a
hundred and thirty different plant species have been identified.

When the winter rains arrive, the desert grasses and shrubs
turn the landscape into emerald patches. This vegetation provides
rich grazing for goats, sheep, and camels. In addition, many small
plants explode in a kaleidoscope of colorful flowers. Their exotic
colors include crimson, orange, yellow, and purple—all colors that
attract insects for pollination. In the past, Bedouin herdsmen

Above: The white Arabian oryx, a rare type of gazelle, was once thought to be extinct from overhunting. A few were found at zoos around the world, and herds of this endangered species have since been built up in Qatar, other Arabian countries, and the United States.
Right: Hunting falcons are kept indoors when they are not being used to hunt rabbits, birds, and other animals.
Below: Such insects as this big mantis take advantage of what greenery exists in Qatar.

Qatari botanists are propagating endangered plants in greenhouses in order to restock the desert where many plants are disappearing.

(nomads) knew many of these small plants and collected them for their sweet scents.

Animal life in the desert is restricted by the environment. The most common species found across the peninsula is the jerboa, or desert rat. There are also several types of amphibians and reptiles including toads, lizards, sand boas, and turtles.

The major large mammals are members of the antelope family. Although the gazelle is rarely spotted in the wild, there are two unique reserves in Qatar that breed endangered species of gazelle in captivity. The famous white Arabian oryx is also being carefully protected and bred on private estates.

Birds are especially abundant along the coast and on the islands of Qatar. They wade and feed in the shallow coves and inlets. Many migratory birds spend their winters in Qatari waters, including thousands of flamingos and cormorants. Falconry is still a popular sport in Qatar during the winter months when prey is readily available for hunting.

Chapter 2

FOOTPRINTS
IN THE SAND

ARCHEOLOGY

Qatar's location along the western shore of the Persian Gulf has ensured its contact with some of the world's earliest civilizations. Human beings have lived in this part of the world for a very long time. Danish archeologists conducting field research in Qatar around 1960 made some remarkable discoveries. They were able to identify more than two hundred sites where Stone Age humans had lived up to 50,000 years ago. Some of the sites produced very primitive flint tools. Other sites yielded cleavers, hand axes, and rough arrowheads. As their research continued, they discovered beautifully

Evidence of ancient humans living in Qatar has been scratched into the rock.

Bedouin, or nomadic, women shelter from the sun and wind in their tents, which they take down and reassemble as they travel. Such a way of life is mostly a thing of the past in Qatar.

Archeologists study ancient pottery to help describe the lives of the earliest inhabitants of Qatar.

designed arrowheads with barbs. The evidence suggests that early humans were nomadic. They moved from site to site in pursuit of animals, berries, roots, or whatever food was available. There wasn't enough food in one place to allow them to settle permanently.

A climate change in Qatar took place 7,000 to 8,000 years ago, bringing more rainfall to the area. Plant and animal life flourished. By 5000 B.C., the new environment attracted a group of people from the valley of the Tigris and Euphrates Rivers in present-day Iraq. These people, known as the Ubaid Culture, were much more advanced than the earlier inhabitants of Qatar. They designed and produced some of the finest flint arrowheads found in Qatar. They were accomplished artists and craftsmen who produced distinctive pottery, as well. The pots were designed with rims and painted geometric patterns. The Ubaids were one of the earliest cultures to abandon the nomadic hunter-gatherer way of life in favor of settlement. The Ubaids may have lived in Qatar for close to one thousand years before decreasing rainfall forced them to leave.

There is little significant evidence of human presence in Qatar for several centuries after the end of the Ubaid period. That does not mean that all human activity on the peninsula ceased. In all likelihood, the Sumerians (the world's oldest civilization, started

This bronze statue is from the Seleucid Empire, which thrived in Syria and adjacent lands about 2,300 years ago.

in Iraq) stopped in Qatar on their way to present-day Oman to acquire copper. Also, a small site found by Danish archeologists on the north-western coast contained pottery from the third century B.C. This would have been left by the Seleucid Empire of Syria, which was founded by one of Alexander the Great's generals. There is also documentation that one of Alexander's admirals visited Qatar in 323 B.C. However, records of any significant permanent settlement in Qatar would have to wait until the religion of Islam was introduced into the area.

For most of the past two thousand years, Qatar has not been a place that attracted large numbers of people. Estimates of the native population even as late as 1950 placed the number of inhabitants at less than 25,000. The environment was harsh and unforgiving. The interior was hot and dry, and there were no major oases where people and livestock could obtain water. The coastline did not have an attractive harbor, and water wells often produced brackish water that was unpleasant to drink. Other Arabs described Qatar as "the land that God forgot." Little did they know that beneath this barren land a secret that would forever change the country and its people was waiting to be discovered.

At the time of Jesus, the only visible resource that this sparse landscape appeared to possess was a brief explosion of vegetation during the winter months when a rainfall of 2 to 3 inches (5 to 7.5 centimeters) turned natural depressions into patches of green. It

Bedouin leaders, or chiefs, are descendants of nomads who led their people to settle in small villages along the coasts many centuries ago.

was this scarce source of vegetation that attracted the desert people of Arabia for a few short months each year. These Bedouin people of Arabia and beyond moved with the rhythm of the seasons. More than twenty different groups are known to have grazed their camels, sheep, and goats in Qatar. It was the nomadic Arabs who would eventually settle the coastal areas and help shape the history of this tiny peninsula in the Persian Gulf.

The fact that some Bedouin settled in small villages along the coast was no surprise. Many Bedouin were not only experts in raising livestock, but were also involved in sailing, fishing, and pearling. It was not uncommon for a nomad to follow his herd during the winter grazing season and to engage in fishing and pearling in the summer months. It was attraction to the mysterious pearl that led many nomads to give up their annual migrations.

Zubarah on the northwest coast was a major Islamic settlement in the conversion of the Middle East to Islam. Though destroyed in the 1800s, its location and importance were commemorated in the 1930s with this replica of the fort that once stood nearby.

THE ISLAMIC ERA

The beginning of the seventh century signaled an event that would change the political, social, and spiritual nature of Qatar forever. The birth of Islam in the commercial center of Mecca in west-central Arabia marked the beginning of modern history in the gulf region. This new religion, founded by the Prophet Muhammad, emphasized a return to the teachings of Abraham. Like Judaism and Christianity, the religion was strongly mono-theistic (belief in one God) and stressed human submission to God's will (the name *Islam* means "submission").

As the Prophet Muhammad preached his message, conversion

The people of Qatar have long been Islamic, with a deep deovition to their faith. This mosque, or Islamic house of worship, is at Al-Wakrah, the second-largest city, located not far from Doha.

to this new faith spread like wildfire across the Arabian Peninsula. After the Prophet's death, the religion of Islam spread across North Africa, southern Europe, the Middle East, and on to southeast Asia. The nomadic Bedouin visiting Qatar brought their new religion and quickly converted the settled people. The Islamic faith continues to be the central pillar in the lives of Qatari citizens.

The ruins of ancient Islamic settlements can be found in many of the coastal areas of Qatar. Al-Huwaila is located among the coastal dunes on the northeast corner of the peninsula. Along the northwest coast near Zubarah are the ruins of Murwah. Recent excavations reveal that Murwah was typical of early Islamic settlements. It appears that there was a fort surrounded by a grouping of about one hundred houses. The discovery of a coin dated A.D. 588, as well as copper artifacts from the same period, suggests that the community had contact with the Arab Abbasid Empire in Baghdad. The inhabitants of this village probably provided pearls to wealthy Baghdad, where they were very much in demand.

Over the next few centuries, the inhabitants of Qatar followed their daily routines. Life changed little, and most people struggled to maintain a simple existence. The Persian Gulf was a highway for the commercial trade moving back and forth across its waters. The people of Qatar were mostly observers of a healthy trade between Asia, the Middle East, and Europe. Even if they had looked, they would not have seen the dark clouds of European imperialism gathering on the horizon.

THE EUROPEANS COME

In 1498, Vasco da Gama sailed from Portugal, around Cape Horn, to India. He was guided across the Indian Ocean by a famous Arab navigator, Ahmad Ibn Majid of Oman. This trip

introduced the Portuguese to the rich trade in the gulf. In 1507, Alfonso de Albuquerque, a Portuguese nobleman and adventurer, captured the fortress at the trading center of Hormuz, which

Life in the Persian Gulf began to change in the fifteenth century when ships from Europe reached its shores.

guarded the entrance to the gulf. The
Portuguese then moved into the gulf
and established a fortress on the
island of Bahrain.

The Portuguese came as
conquerors. They demanded heavy
taxes and treated the people badly.
Their treatment of prisoners was
particularly harsh. Occasionally they
cut off the noses and ears of the men they
captured. The evil reputation they acquired slowed trade
in the gulf, and all of the countries, including Qatar, suffered.

The Portuguese stayed in the gulf for more than a century.
Eventually, they came into conflict with the British who had
established a foothold in India in 1600. Annoyed by Portuguese
interference with their trade in the gulf, the British responded. In
April 1622, the British navy, along with Persian troops, captured
Hormuz and ended Portuguese domination of the Persian Gulf
region. The English became the superior power.

Most of the gulf region, including Qatar, was broken up into
areas under the control of a leader, or prince, called a *sheikh*
(pronounced "shake"). The British did not interfere much with the
sheikhdoms. They were content to build their empire in India and
to enjoy the large profits made by expanding trade opportunities.

This fort in Muscat, Oman, southeast of Qatar, was typical of the forts built by the Portuguese in the heyday of their exploration and control of the region.

The main British policy centered on keeping the gulf shipping lanes open. Cotton, teak, tobacco, pearls, tea, raw silk, spices, and a multitude of other items moved through the gulf and on to Europe. In 1753, the British established a British Political Resident at Bushire, Persia (now Iran), to oversee their commercial and security interests. They were unaware that events unfolding in Qatar would have a significant impact on their role in the gulf.

During the early 1700s, two ethnic groups that would help shape Qatar's modern history migrated to the peninsula. The Utubs settled in the northwest corner of the country near Zubarah. The Tamim settled along the east coast near present-day Doha. The Al-Khalifah family of the Utub tribe and the Al-Thani family of the Tamim would, for the next two centuries, engage in a power struggle for control of Qatar.

Ruins of the one of the old Al-Thani family castles lie near Umm Salal Mohammed, a few miles north of Doha.

TWO FAMILIES

The Utub stayed in Qatar only a short time before continuing on to Kuwait. In Kuwait, the Utub became very successful merchants and pearl traders. As the tribe grew in numbers, the Al-Khalifah family decided to return to Qatar. In 1766 the Al-Khalifahs settled at Zubarah, on the northwest coast of Qatar. The group was led by Sheikh Ahmad bin Muhammad ibn Khalifah and his five sons. A wise and respected leader, Sheikh Ahmad had accumulated considerable wealth as a pearl trader. At once, he used some of his wealth to build a well-equipped fort facing the sea. Then he built a wall around the city to protect the inhabitants from attack.

Visitors to Qatar's shores would have found people living in huts made of palm fronds, called barasti *huts.*

Other merchants and traders flocked to Zubarah. In a short time, the city became a prosperous port and commercial center. The city began to rival Bahrain as a trade center, and Bahrain's inhabitants became jealous of Zubarah. A series of incidents led to Bahrain attacking Zubarah. As the siege on Zubarah worsened, Sheikh Ahmad sent for help from some of the powerful Bedouin groups in the area. They accepted the call to battle and helped save Zubarah. Later, the combined forces of the Al-Khalifah and the Bedouin attacked Bahrain, defeating the island's forces. In 1783 Sheikh Ahmad bin Muhammad ibn Khalifah became the ruler of Bahrain. More than two hundred years later, the Al-Khalifah family still rules Bahrain.

Most of the family and many of the Bedouin stayed on the island to share the spoils of victory. A few returned to Zubarah, discontented with their share of the spoils. The Al-Khalifah never gave up their claim to Zubarah, a claim that would eventually lead to conflict with the Al-Thani family of the Tamim tribe.

The Al-Thani family settled primarily along the eastern coast of Qatar. Their sheikhs were in control of a number of small villages from Al-Khor in the north, to Khor al-Udaid in the south. They

During an era when piracy was a worldwide phenomenon on the seas, Qatar, too, had its pirates on the Persian Gulf, interfering with British trade. This dramatic drawing of the era was based on Mediterranean pirates.

engaged primarily in livestock grazing and pearling. They had little contact with European imperialists in the gulf until the early 1800s. Finally, the Al-Thani were brought into contact with the British because of the increasing activity of pirates in the gulf.

Piracy was not new to the world's shipping lanes. The British themselves had encouraged pirates to attack Spanish ships in the New World. However, they were disturbed by the actions of pirates from the gulf sheikhdoms, including Qatar. Piracy was interfering with trade in the gulf, something the British would not tolerate.

The pirates considered themselves to be engaged in an honorable profession. They viewed capturing ships and stealing

The Arab boat called the dhow *moved through the Persian Gulf and the Red Sea with ease, making piracy a way of life for some Qataris.*

their goods as a reasonable source of livelihood from the sea. In general, the sailors of captured ships were not exposed to any great violence, once they had surrendered. While engaged in the fight, however, no quarter was given. The pirates knew they were in a risky business. If they lost, they expected no mercy.

The most famous pirate known in the gulf in modern times was Sheikh Rahmah ibn Jabir of Qatar. Not an Al-Thani, he operated out of a base at Khor Hasan, north of Zubarah. His tribe squabbled with the Al-Khalifah of Bahrain, and he maintained a lifelong hatred for them. For more than forty years, he plundered the trading ships of Bahrain. A European traveler who met Sheikh Rahmah when he was an old man described his appearance as a threatening sight. "His body was lanky and thin. His arms and legs had been cut and hacked, and pierced with the wounds of sabers, spears, and bullets. His face was naturally ferocious and ugly, covered with many scars, and one eye was missing."

The dhow is still an important craft in the Persian Gulf, and taking care of it has changed little over the centuries. This man is caulking his dhow.

The British were eager to rid the gulf of pirates in order to protect their trade routes. They were convinced that the sheikhdom called Ras Al-Khaimah (now a part of the United Arab Emirates) was the center of pirate activity. In 1819 they attacked Ras al-Khaimah and set fire to the boats they believed were engaged in piracy. In January 1820, the British signed a treaty with the sheikhs of the Lower Gulf and Bahrain to establish peace. The General Treaty called for an end to piracy, arms smuggling, and the slave trade by the Arabs. Events in the interior were to be of no concern to the British. A representative from Qatar was not invited to sign the General Treaty. Qatar would eventually pay a heavy price for this omission, and the Al-Thani would have a rude introduction to the British.

British response to any report of piracy was swift and massive. In 1821 a British ship severely bombarded the town of Doha as punishment for an alleged act of piracy. Since the people of Qatar had not been aware of the treaty, they had no idea why they were being subjected to such a brutal attack. When the British Political Resident from Bushire called on Doha a year later, he found the residents still puzzled by the vicious attack. After discussion, the Al-Thani family leaders agreed to abide by the rules of the General Treaty. This contact set the stage for the British participation in Qatar's internal affairs for the next one hundred and fifty years. However, the Al-Thani would have to balance other attacks on their sovereignty from the Wahhabis, the Ottoman Turks, and Bahrain.

THE WAHHABIS

The Wahhabis were from central Arabia near Riyadh. They were followers of a political-religious alliance between Muhammad ibn Abd al-Wahhab and Muhammad ibn Saud. Abd al-Wahhab was a religious reformer who preached a return to the fundamental beliefs of Islam. Muhammad ibn Saud would become ruler of a large portion of the Arabian Peninsula. Together, they set out to conquer and purify Saudi Arabia. By 1795, they had also conquered Qatar. However, they held control only a short time. They would return again in the 1850s, but their impact would be more religious than political. The first Al-Thani sheikh to rule Qatar, Muhammad bin Thani, established close ties with the Wahhabis of Riyadh. This alliance gave him a powerful friend in his long-running feud with Bahrain.

Muhammad bin Thani's support of the Wahhabis was not well received in Bahrain. The Al-Khalifahs of Bahrain had continued to demand a payment of tribute from the Al-Thani. In addition, the Al-Khalifahs did not like the strict religion preached by the

Dariyah (right) was the original home of Muhammad ibn Saud, who championed the reformist beliefs of Muhammad ibn Abd al-Wahhab and founded the strict Wahhabi variety of Islam. Shown above is an heir to the Ibn Saud throne in 1928, with his counselors.

Wahhabi. In 1867 the Al-Thani refused to pay their tribute to Bahrain. Bahrain reacted quickly. They solicited the support of the sheikh of Abu Dhabi, who also had a long-running grudge with the Al-Thani over a border dispute. Together, they launched a devastating attack on Doha and Al-Wakrah, literally blotting these cities from existence. Only those residents who fled to the interior of the peninsula escaped with their lives.

As soon as they could rally their forces, the Qataris launched a courageous counterattack on Bahrain. Hundreds were killed, without a clear victory for either side. Tension was high and peace was threatened in the gulf. Again, the British would not tolerate

A Portuguese fort built on the island of Bahrain is being restored as a museum. It may have suffered some damage during the Qatari attack on Bahrain during the nineteenth century.

conditions that might harm their commerce. They responded early in 1868.

The British Political Resident at Bushire, Lewis Pelly, sailed to Bahrain, determined to stop the conflict. He pointed out that Bahrain had seriously violated the treaty they had signed with the British just seven years before. In that treaty, Bahrain had agreed to abstain from aggressive acts on the sea, and promised not to start a war with its neighbors. Bahrain had clearly violated its treaty with Britain, and it must pay the penalty. Pelly forced the ruling sheikh of Bahrain, Muhammad ibn Khalifah, to step down and replaced him with his brother. Then he destroyed Sheikh Muhammad's palace-fortress on Muharraq Island and burned his war fleet.

As soon as he was finished in Bahrain, Pelly left for Qatar, where he met with Muhammad bin Thani. There he requested that Sheikh Muhammad sign an agreement guaranteeing not to engage in war at sea. This agreement was Qatar's first step toward independence. The most important British official in the Persian Gulf area had recognized the Al-Thani as the legitimate rulers of Qatar.

OTTOMAN TURKS

The next threat to interference in Qatar's internal affairs came from the Ottoman Turks in 1871. The Ottoman Empire, though declining in power, still controlled a considerable portion of the eastern Mediterranean. Its representatives requested that Qatar acknowledge their position of power in the region and fly the Turkish flag. By that time, Sheikh Muhammad was advanced in years and had begun to share official duties with his son, Qasim bin Muhammad Al-Thani. The old sheikh hated the Turks and refused to fly their flag. But young Sheikh Qasim agreed to fly the Turkish flag over his fort. It was a very clever decision. The Turks would establish only a small presence, interfering little in the day-to-day affairs of state. Sheikh Qasim could use their presence to balance British influence and to prevent the Bahrainis from trying to dominate.

The Crescent and Star, still seen on Turkey's flag, were the symbols of the powerful Ottoman Empire as it tried to spread its influence throughout the entire Middle East and Mediterranean region.

Doha Fort, built in the nineteenth century, served the Qatari people during their final confrontations with the Ottoman forces. Today it is a museum.

Sheikh Qasim's next step was to secure his position on the northwest coast, which the Al-Khalifahs of Bahrain still claimed as their domain. In 1878, he attacked Zubarah and wiped it off the map. Finally, the entire peninsula was in the hands of the Al-Thani. Sheikh Qasim had proved to be a great warrior. Now he could turn his attention to ruling Qatar.

Sheikh Qasim would have little time to enjoy his success, however. The Turks, who had originally interfered little in Qatari internal affairs, started to become a nuisance. They had plans to take over more of the decision-making process each day. Worse yet, they had begun to demand a tribute that was excessive. Whenever he could, Sheikh Qasim tried to block Turkish moves for expansion.

Finally, in 1893, the Ottoman governor of Basra visited Doha with a regiment of infantry and three hundred cavalry in a show of force. Sheikh Qasim left Doha and sought refuge inland. The Ottoman governor blocked all exits by land and sea and marched toward the fortress where Sheikh Qasim had taken refuge. The situation appeared bleak, and Sheikh Qasim warned his followers

An artist created this view of the way Zubarah looked when it was a thriving commercial center before its destruction in 1878.

to leave or be prepared to die. They stayed and fought a brave battle. In one day of fighting, they defeated the Turks, turning Ottoman Turkish influence in Qatar into a memory. Sheikh Qasim and his men became legendary heroes.

THE TWENTIETH CENTURY

Sheikh Qasim lived in semi-retirement for the rest of his life before passing away in 1913. Before his death, he initiated new programs to unify the country. Roads were built to connect the main towns, and he established ten schools for religious

Many small villages were left to fall into ruins during the twentieth century when villagers moved to the cities to take advantage of Qatar's development.

The majlis, *or meeting room, of Sheikh Abdullah bin Qasim Al-Thani, who ruled from 1913 to 1949, was where official discussions were held. The building is now part of the Qatar National Museum.*

instruction. He converted to the conservative branch of Islam, known as Wahhabi, in his later years. Most Qataris followed him in his conversion, and today Qatar is principally a Wahhabi-Islamic society.

Sheikh Qasim was followed by his son, Abdullah. When World War I broke out in Europe, the new sheikh quickly sided with the British. He sent a note to the British Political Resident in Bushire with his wishes for success and ultimate victory. Now that the Ottomans were out of Qatar, the British were interested in securing their position. In November 1916, Sheikh Abdullah signed an exclusive agreement with Britain. It was similar to the Treaty of

This oil well, the first one opened in Qatar, was located in the Dukhan hills. The oil field was not developed until well after World War II, when oil began to radically change the lives of the Qatari citizens.

Maritime Peace in Perpetuity signed by other gulf sheikhdoms in 1853. In the treaty, Abdullah agreed, "not to cede, sell, lease or mortgage any of his territory without British consent; not to have relations with any foreign power without British consent; and to desist from piracy, the slave trade, and arms traffic." The British, in turn, guaranteed to protect Qatar from both land and sea attacks.

Sheikh Abdullah ruled Qatar for a very long time, until 1949. Economic conditions were difficult in the little country. The income from pearls collapsed during the Great Depression in Europe and America. It would never truly recover because, also in the 1930s, the Japanese introduced cultured pearls, which could be acquired much more cheaply than the naturally occurring gems.

Searching for an alternative source of revenue, the country

welcomed the opportunity to develop an oil industry. In May 1935, Sheikh Abdullah signed an agreement with the Iraq Petroleum Company, which was made up of British, Dutch, American, and French interests. Oil was discovered in 1939, near Dukhan, on the western side of the peninsula. However, the long years of World War II delayed development of the oil field. Exports of oil did not begin until 1949.

Sheikh Abdullah abdicated that same year and was followed as emir by his son, Sheikh Ali bin Abdullah Al-Thani. Early in his reign, Sheikh Ali signed a concession to develop offshore oil fields. As the revenue from oil increased, the Al-Thani initiated an organized plan for modernization. A British agent was stationed in Doha, and British and Egyptian advisors helped to establish a modern administrative system.

In 1968, the British stunned the world by announcing the end of British defense agreements east of Suez. They were putting an end to their centuries-long dominance in the Persian Gulf. They said that by 1971 they would terminate all treaties of protection with the gulf sheikhdoms.

The immediate response was to try to establish a federation of Qatar, Bahrain, and the seven sheihkdoms called the Trucial States—Abu Dhabi, Dubai, Sharjah, Ajman, Umm al-Quwain, Ras al-Khaimah, and Fujairah. Leaders of these nine small countries held talks leading to unification. As the deadline for British withdrawal from the region approached, it became apparent that the political marriage of the nine sheikhdoms would not work. Bahrain and Qatar continued to distrust each other, based on centuries of feuding. Strong personalities and the interests of other sheikhdoms created friction in the talks for unification.

Doha Bay, which is dredged regularly to accommodate the huge ships of modern enterprise, symbolizes the changes brought by the discovery of oil in Qatar.

Finally, in 1970, Qatar and Bahrain withdrew from the talks and decided to establish independent nations. The other seven sheikhdoms continued their discussions and went on to form the independent nation of the United Arab Emirates.

As Qatar prepared for independence, the need for strong and decisive leadership became apparent. In 1960 Sheikh Ahmad bin Ali Al-Thani had taken over power from his father, Sheikh Ali. Sheikh Ahmad had a lot of his father's characteristics. He was both religious and intellectual. He loved to collect and read books on Arab history and Islamic law. He was especially fond of hunting with falcons. The boredom of everyday administrative tasks held little interest for him. He turned over most of the administrative duties to his cousin, Sheikh Khalifah bin Hamad Al-Thani. Sheikh Khalifah became the driving force behind the movement for independence and the birth of a modern nation.

Above: Sheikh Khalifah bin Hamad Al-Thani oversaw the profound changes that came to Qatar during his reign from 1972 to 1995.
Right: His son, Sheikh Hamad bin Khalifah Al-Thani, became the emir of Qatar in 1995, when he and his advisors felt that Qatar needed a new approach to the future.

Chapter 3

BIRTH OF A NATION

If Qatar can be said to have "a father," it would be Sheikh Khalifah bin Hamad Al-Thani. Born in 1932, he was destined to become a great leader. One of the favorite grandsons of the wise and aged Sheikh Abdullah, Sheikh Khalifah showed early signs of leadership potential. Growing up, young Khalifah knew that his father, Sheikh Hamad, would assume leadership of the country ahead of him, but Sheikh Hamad died unexpectedly in 1948. Khalifah's uncle and then a cousin became the leader of Qatar.

However, Sheikh Khalifah had already had considerable training in how to be an effective leader. Like his father, Sheikh Khalifah was wise, pious, energetic, and possessed a powerful personality. He showed an early interest in helping to govern the country. At nineteen, he assumed his first public office as director of police and internal security. In 1953, he served as a judge in a court of law in Doha. Then he went on to become director of education, minister of finance and petroleum affairs, and finally Prime minister and deputy ruler. He had more than twenty years of administrative experience before he assumed power in 1972.

BASIC LAW OF 1970

One of Sheikh Khalifah's major responsibilities was to help guide Qatar to independence. He played a key role in drafting a provisional constitution. The Basic Law of 1970 was published on April 2, 1970, becoming the temporary constitution for the nation. Qatar was the first nation of the sheikhdoms in the Lower Gulf to adopt a written constitution.

The original constitution was composed of seventy-seven Articles. It declared that Qatar was a sovereign and independent state. Islam was the official religion of the country. Shar'ia (Islamic Law) was the principal source of legislation. Democracy was the basis for the system of government, and Arabic was the official language.

The new constitution also required that the ruler of Qatar had to be an Al-Thani. However, any new ruler was to be chosen only after a process of consultation with family and other leaders. The ruler possessed supreme power over executive and legislative decisions with advice from a Council of Ministers and an Advisory Council. Judicial matters fell in the domain of Shar'ia courts and civil courts. The constitution also provided that the title of the ruler would be "Emir of Qatar."

The most important provision in the new constitution required the formation of a State Advisory Council. In Arabic, it is called the *Majlis a'Shura.* The council was to be composed of individuals from three different sources including the ministers of all administrative departments. Select members of the ruling Al-Thani family would also serve on the council. Twenty members would be appointed by the emir from a group of forty candidates chosen in a public election. The candidates were to be elected from all regions of the country and represent a wide range of interest groups. In 1975, the number of elected representatives was increased from twenty to thirty members.

The new Emiri Palace, or Diwan, *is the seat of government in Qatar. The emir holds weekly audiences, a meeting called the Majlis, with his advisors.*

The State Advisory Council reflected the long-standing principles of what is referred to as "desert democracy." Tribal political organization was based on a strong central leader who consulted with his tribal elders before making a decision. Consensus, or general agreement, within the group shaped the leader's decisions. Today that same consensus from the Advisory Council shapes the decisions of the emir. The Advisory Council debates general policy, including administrative, economic, or political matters. They debate laws proposed by the Council of Ministers before they are submitted to the emir for ratification. The Council may request that a minister explain his policies, and the members are responsible for reviewing the annual budget.

INDEPENDENCE AND LEADERSHIP

With a temporary constitution in place, Sheikh Khalifah was now ready to move to independence. His cousin, Sheikh Ahmad,

Qatar plays an active role in Middle Eastern affairs. Here, Foreign Minister Hamad Bin Jasem (right) met in 1995 with Palestine Liberation Organization leader Yasser Arafat (center) and U.S. Secretary of State Warren Christopher (left).

was still the official ruler, but Sheikh Khalifah was the major force in preparing Qatar for independence. On September 1, 1971, Qatar was recognized as an independent nation. A few days later, it became a full member of the United Nations and the Arab League.

The fact that the emir of the new nation, Sheikh Ahmad, had made the announcement of independence from his villa in Geneva, Switzerland, was unpopular in Qatar. He was spending too much time out of the country and seemed to have little interest in governing. In addition, he made no attempt to create the Advisory Council that the new constitution called for.

After lengthy consultations, the Al-Thani family decided to depose Sheikh Ahmad. On February 22, 1972, Sheikh Khalifah bin Hamad Al-Thani assumed leadership of the country with the full support of the ruling family, the people of Qatar, and the armed forces. Sheikh Khalifah would rule over a golden era in the history of Qatar. His energy and dynamic leadership would reshape the country's direction.

As the new emir of Qatar, Sheikh Khalifah moved quickly to initiate the reforms he had promised. One of his first steps was to establish the Advisory Council decreed by the constitution. His next step was to increase the salaries of the civil servants and the armed forces to encourage efficiency and to secure his position. He terminated the previous practice of one-quarter of the nation's oil revenues going directly to the ruler's personal bank account. Instead, he directed that this money go to the government treasury for the welfare of all Qatari citizens. He made a commitment to the nation to provide free education, health care, utilities, and public housing, as well as employment and security. The reforms that he initiated and the development programs he carried out totally transformed the nation.

In 1977 Sheikh Khalifah signed a decree appointing his son, Sheikh Hamad bin Khalifah Al-Thani, as heir apparent and minister of defense. For almost two decades, Sheikh Hamad served as the second-ranking decision-maker in Qatar. He possessed the same type of energy and administrative abilities as his father. Hand in hand, they worked together to build an efficient government. When his father was absent, Sheikh Hamad took over the reins of government. He studied his father's leadership carefully, preparing for the time when he would be called on to govern. Gradually, he took over more and more responsibility.

In June 1995, Sheikh Hamad quietly deposed his father after he had ruled for more than twenty-three years. It was time for a change of leadership, and once again the family, the citizens of Qatar, and the armed forces supported the change.

Sheikh Hamad has proved to be an innovative and modern leader in the short time he has been emir. He has scheduled municipal elections, loosened restrictions on the press, and encouraged the citizens of Qatar to prepare for more participation in the government. He has also held foreign policy discussions with government ministers from neighboring Iran and Iraq, and he has attempted to normalize relations with Israel.

In late 1996, the emir appointed his eighteen-year-old son, Jassem bin Hamad Al-Thani as the heir apparent. A recent graduate of Sandhurst Military Academy in Britain, Sheikh Jassem is active in the army of Qatar. A quiet, handsome, and intelligent young man, Sheikh Jassem shows signs of great leadership ability. His mother, Sheikha Mozea Al-Misnad, is active in educational reform and social issues.

MILITARY

Qatar maintains a modest defense force, as would be expected of a small nation. It has an army, navy, and air force composed of approximately ten thousand military personnel. The troops are highly trained and combat-ready.

The Qatari military is part of a regional defense program that includes Saudi Arabia, Bahrain, Kuwait, Oman, and the United Arab Emirates. Armed forces from these countries frequently engage in joint military-training exercises. When their neighbor Kuwait was illegally invaded by Iraq, Qatar reacted immediately in condemning the invasion. Qatari troops participated in both Desert Shield and Desert Storm, the United Nations' programs to force Iraq out of Kuwait. The troops distinguished themselves in battle and won the admiration of other countries.

The country also maintains a police and civil defense force of

Girls and boys in Qatar attend separate schools. Girls wear uniforms at the primary school shown above. At right, a schoolboy gets some help from his teacher in reading the Qur'an. Religion is taught in all the public schools.

about seven thousand members. Crime is very rare in Qatar, and visitors feel a wonderful sense of security. Individuals can walk alone on the streets at night with no fear of being attacked. Drug and alcohol abuse are almost non-existent. Security and safety for the family is a guiding social principle in Qatar.

EDUCATION

Education was difficult to acquire when Qatar was a small, poor country. Boys and girls had many responsibilities—tending livestock, mending fishing nets, learning to cook, and helping to care for younger children. Because the religion of Islam is so central to life in Qatar, the first schools were religious schools.

Children in Qatar, like children everywhere, enjoy field trips. These students are learning about the newly built computerized post office in the capital of Doha.

Students learned to recite verses from the Holy Qur'an, or Koran. They were taught reading, writing, and Shar'ia lessons.

Then came the modernization of the country as all Qatari citizens began to share in the wealth generated from oil and gas sales. The first public primary school was established in 1952. Four years later, the government formed an education ministry, and modernization continued rapidly. Today, more than 98 percent of all children attend school, although education is not compulsory. Children begin primary school at six years of age and continue for six years. When they are twelve, they begin three years of preparatory school before completing their education with three years of secondary school.

Boys and girls go to separate schools in Qatar. The leaders of the nation believe this is best for their children. Students study the typical courses, including math, language, science, and social studies. They also study religion. Students are very polite and

A chemistry student at the University of Qatar performs an experiment in the modern laboratory.

well-mannered, showing great respect for their teachers. They also have fun, playing soccer, their favorite sport, at recess, and going on field trips to historical sites, museums, the post office, and other government offices.

There are also private schools to educate the children of foreign workers. The British, French, Indian, Japanese, Lebanese, Norwegian, and Americans who come to Qatar to work all provide private schools for their children. Their courses are approved by the Ministry of Education, and boys and girls are allowed to go to school together. Some Qatari parents send their children to these private schools so they have the opportunity to learn other languages, especially English. Everyone who attends the private schools must pay tuition.

The University of Qatar was established by the emir's decree in 1977. In 1985 it was moved to a new campus that is noted for its unique architecture. The buildings are designed to reflect traditional Arab and Islamic shapes. Many of the buildings are octagons, with wind towers. The wind tower was an ancient design that allows a breeze to flow through the building during

The spectacular new campus of the University of Qatar uses an ancient design incorporating wind towers that put even the slightest breeze to work cooling the buildings.

the hottest part of the summer. The campus also has several courtyards with fountains and beautiful gardens.

University students are also separated into a boys' campus and a girls' campus. There are more girls enrolled at the university than boys. The girls frequently select education as a major and go on to careers in teaching. The boys usually study business, hoping for a career in government service or private industry. The university provides generous scholarships for students from other Arab and Islamic countries.

A beautiful mosque is located next to the university library, so that students can attend daily prayers. Sports are important, too, with athletes from the University of Qatar competing with athletes from the other five GCC (Gulf Cooperation Council) countries.

Education from the first grade through college is completely free in Qatar. The nation provides all of the textbooks, paper, transportation, sports clothes, and other necessities at all levels of education. For many years, the state has spent almost 10 percent of its budget on education. This was a result of Sheikh Khalifah's belief that the children of Qatar are the nation's most valuable asset. As such, he believed that their potential should be developed to the fullest extent.

HEALTH CARE

The level of health care in Qatar is excellent. The average citizen can expect to live more than seventy years. This places their life expectancy on a par with Western industrial nations. Health care is provided free of charge to anyone living in Qatar. Even non-citizens benefit from the program provided by the nation.

Health centers are widely distributed, and a patient is never more than a few miles from immediate medical care. Each health center is staffed with a full medical team. The center has family doctors, specialists, nurses, laboratory technicians, and a pharmacy. If the patient is diagnosed to have a serious problem, he or she will be transported to the Hamad Medical Corporation facility in Doha.

The Hamad Medical Corporation has three separate hospitals that provide some of the best health care in the world. The doctors have been recruited from top medical universities in Great Britain, Syria, Egypt, and many other countries. The diagnostic equipment includes the most modern technology available. There is a special

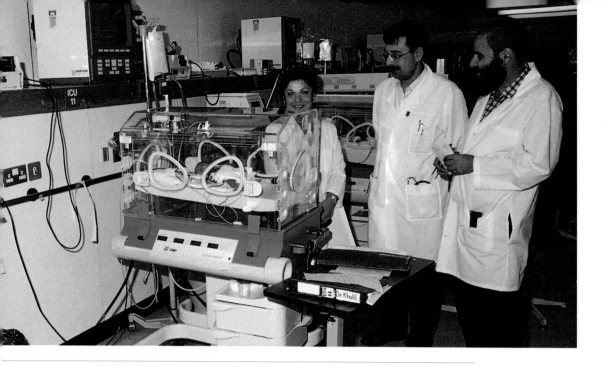

At the Hamad Medical Corporation hospital in Doha, doctors making their rounds examine premature babies in the special nursery.

room where scans can be conducted to identify brain or nerve damage. The trauma unit has saved many lives by responding quickly to the needs of accident victims. The neonatal unit is working miracles at saving the lives of premature babies. Little babies weighing less than 2 pounds (1 kilogram) at birth are carefully monitored twenty-four hours a day to ensure that they will have a fair chance to live.

The Ministry of Public Health encourages mothers to have their children immunized against contagious diseases. The ministry is responsible for measuring water quality and monitoring for contaminated food. Finally, it engages in an active program of public awareness and educational programs to protect and inform all residents of Qatar. The country is on target to meet the challenge of the World Health Organization to ensure: "Health for all by the year 2000."

PUBLIC HOUSING

No nation has been more generous with its public housing projects than Qatar. Since 1973, more than 10,000 houses have been built by the government for people with limited financial resources. A poor citizen of Qatar can buy one of these "popular houses" if he is married, is between twenty and fifty years old, and cannot afford to build his own house.

The government gives him a free piece of land. It allows him to borrow the money to build his home without having to pay interest on the loan. He is required to pay back only 60 percent of the original loan in easy payments over a twenty-five-year period. The government pays the full costs of insuring the house and gives the homeowner a generous amount of money to buy furniture. If the homeowner dies or is disabled, his wife and children receive the house at no additional cost.

The homes are attractively designed and may be one or two stories high. They are located in pleasant new suburbs. Each house has four bedrooms, a living room, den, dining room, kitchen, two and a half baths, laundry and storage room, and a garage.

These one-story houses are at Al-Ruwais at the northern end of the peninsula.

Fabric stores now come in two styles: the old shop in the souq, or traditional market (above), and the newer store in a modern mall, where buyers can examine the goods in leisure and comfort.

Chapter 4

THE ECONOMY —
OLD AND NEW

The story of Qatar's economic life is sharply divided into the era before the discovery of oil and gas and the time after its discovery. The difference is like night and day. Prior to the discovery of valuable mineral fuels, Qatar was one of the poorest nations in the world. It supported less than 25,000 people. There were no large cities. There was no electricity, running water, or organized health care. The few roads that existed were little more than dirt paths that wound through poor little villages built of mud and stick huts. Education was almost nonexistent except for a few religious schools.

Today Qatar is one of the richest nations in the world. Four-lane superhighways stretch from Doha, the capital, to other important centers. Power-generation plants crank out hundreds of megawatts of electricity. Huge machinery converts seawater to fresh water. Doha has been transformed into a beautiful, modern city. The nation's population has grown to more than half a million people.

To understand the change that has taken place, we must first look at the old economy. It was an economic system based on nomadic grazing, fishing, pearling, and trade.

THE BEDOUIN

The Bedouin tribes of Arabia made their annual migrations to Qatar for many centuries. These people, whose name means "desert dweller" in Arabic, moved herds of camels, sheep, and goats during the winter months when rains produced life-supporting grasses and desert shrubs in Qatar. Some of the tribes would travel up to 700 miles (1,120 kilometers) in search of new vegetation, traveling 30 to 40 miles (48 to 64 kilometers) each day. After they reached the winter pastures, the pace could become more relaxed. They made short moves every few days following the grazing livestock. As the vegetation turned brown and began to die with the change in seasons, the Bedouin drifted back to their summer camps in Arabia. They were visitors rather than permanent residents.

Gradually a pattern of change began to evolve. In northern and eastern Qatar, the Bedouin settled in small villages along the coast and engaged in two different occupations. In the summers, the men went to sea to dive for oysters that might contain the pearls valued by people the world over. In the winters, they herded their livestock from temporary camps in the interior of the peninsula. The vegetation in the north was well suited for sheep and goats. Although they kept a few camels, the donkey was the common beast of burden.

Life was simple. Along the coast they lived in *barasti,* huts made of palm fronds and thatch. When they went to the interior, they lived in tents that they carried with them. The men and boys did the herding and notched the animals' ears for identification. Men also slaughtered the animals for meat. The women of the tribe

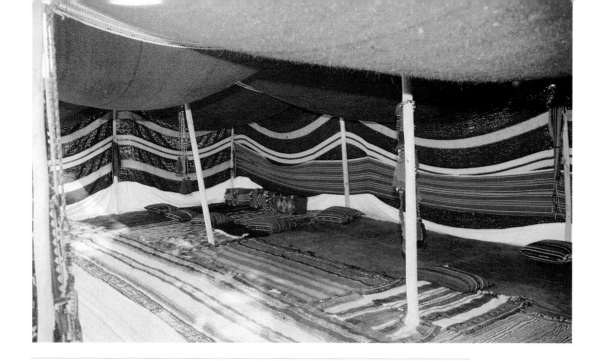

A traditional Bedouin tent was lined with colorful blankets that were easy to fold and move.

did the milking and made dairy products. They also wove traditional cloth with wool. The most prominent tribe in the north was the Al-Na'im. After the discovery of oil, most northern Bedouin abandoned livestock grazing and drifted into the cities to work.

In southern Qatar, Bedouin life was much more traditional. Frequently on the move, the desert dwellers lived in camps of seven to ten tents. The tents were made of hand-woven camel hair and were usually black or brown in color. The side facing south was always left open to catch the soft, warm breezes that came from that direction. The Bedouin also knew that strong, violent winds (the *shamal*) blew from the north. The north wind was accompanied by blowing sand and dust, making zero visibility. The wise Bedouin sought cover when the shamal came.

In camp, the duties were well established. Daily life was guided by age and gender. Although it was seldom expressed,

Some Bedouin still prefer living in their tents—at least part of the time—but they are more likely to travel in a Range Rover than with camels.

male dominance existed at all age levels. Great respect was always shown for elders, a tradition that continues in much of Arab society today. Children commonly sat at the feet of their elders and listened patiently to stories and poems. The Bedouin were great poets and storytellers.

The women were responsible for setting up and breaking down the camp. They packed the pots and pans, folded the tents, and loaded the pack camels. When a new camp had been established, their major responsibility was food preparation. They gathered twigs, branches, and dried camel manure for their fires. The women were also talented weavers. They combed the camel hair or wool of the sheep and goats and spun it into yarn. Then with simple looms they wove beautiful blankets and cloth fabric. The Bedouin cloth called Al-Sadw is still made today.

The men's main responsibility was to take care of the camels. An individual family would own a herd composed of forty to fifty adult females. There would be three or four males for breeding purposes. In addition, there were always a few camels trained for

In the past, Bedouin bred their camels and perhaps brought extra ones to be sold at a livestock market.

riding or used as beasts of burden. The birth of a female camel was cause for great rejoicing. The milk of the female was the mainstay of the Bedouin diet. Young male calves were slaughtered for their sweet and tender meat. It was frequently served on occasions when honored guests were present.

The Bedouin herdsman had a special affection for his camels. Each camel was given a name, and most would come when called. Whenever the herdsman worked with a camel, he petted it, talked to it, or sang to it constantly. The camels were milked twice daily, in the morning before they left camp to graze, and again when they returned to camp in the evening.

The camel was the dominant force in the Bedouin's life. Its milk and meat provided the main source of food. Its hair was used for making tents and cloth. Sometimes women made camel-hair foot coverings to protect the family's feet from the scorching sands of the desert. The skin was used to make leather bags for carrying water. The dried manure was a common fuel for the cooking fires. Even the urine was collected and used to cure leather and for washing hair. The urine was a natural treatment for removing head lice from children's hair.

The Bedouin seldom visit south Qatar today. Like the cowboys in the Old West, they are more legend than reality. However, their tradition of hospitality, loyalty, bravery, respect, and patience are woven into Qatari society. If they do go to the desert for vacation or week-end camping, they no longer travel by camel, the famed "ship of the desert." Instead, four-wheel-drive Land Rovers, Nissans, and Toyotas are the preferred mode of transportation. The "romantic" nomadic life is now the subject of television programs from Doha and the dreams of the youthful generation. The United States has "urban cowboys." Qatar has "urban Bedouin."

THE SEA

Qatar is a peninsula surrounded by the sea on three sides. It has more than 350 miles (563 kilometers) of coastline. It was only natural that early visitors were attracted to the sea by its rich bounty of fish. For those individuals who settled along the coast, fish was the major food in their diet. Fish was an excellent source of protein. Rice with fish was eaten almost daily.

In ancient times, most boats were built from wood, but Qatar had no forests. A few palm trees could be found along the coast and in gardens where wells were available. The original boats in

Fishermen repair their fish traps in order to keep catching the abundant fish found in the sea around Qatar.

Qatar were made of palm fronds. These long leaves measured about 12 to 15 feet (3.5 to 4.5 meters) in length. The boats were shaped like today's canoes, only they were a little wider. They were not very stable, so it was dangerous to fish in high winds. The shamal from the north could produce waves 12 feet (3.5 meters) high. The fishermen shared stories about boats being eaten by the sea. Many a man lost his life while trying to earn a livelihood from the sea.

As boat construction improved, Arab boatbuilders began to make boats from wood. By the time the Portuguese arrived in the Persian Gulf, the trusty dhow was a common sight. This kind of boat was 30 to 50 feet (9 to 15 meters) in length and made of teak-wood planks imported from India. The teak planks were sewn together with coconut fiber. The cracks between the planks were stuffed, or caulked, with rope to prevent the boat from leaking. Whenever the boats were in harbor, sailors would caulk the hull to repair leaks. The dhows were powered by the wind with two large sails. They also had a shallow draft so they could dock in bays where the water was not deep.

Traditional dhows are tied up at this very nontraditional Taco Bell restaurant.

The dhow became the workhorse of the Persian Gulf. It was used for fishing, pearling, and carrying trade goods. Since the interior of Qatar was largely uninhabited desert, many goods needed to be imported. Vegetables came from Persia (Iran), cotton and teak from India, and dates from the Trucial Coast.

This special craft is still being built in the boatyards of Doha using the traditional methods. The design has changed through the years to include some Portuguese concepts. The dhows are larger today, up to 120 feet (36 meters) in length. Instead of coconut binding, the planks are fastened with nails wrapped in oiled fiber to keep the nail from splitting the plank.

It is most remarkable that the work of dhow-building is done without plans or drawings. Measurements are made by eye alone, along with years of experience on the part of a master craftsman. While the dhow is still used in gulf trade and fishing, it gained its fame during the era of pearling.

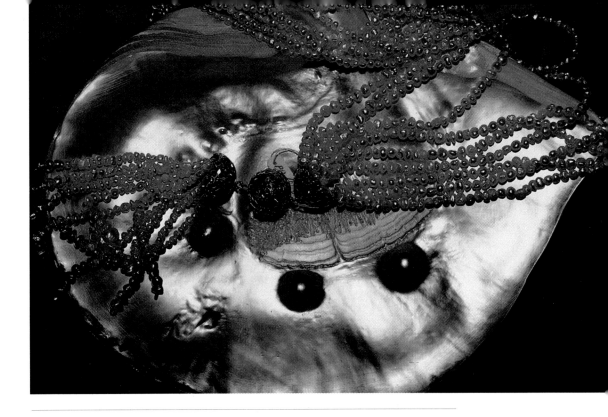

The inside of an oyster shell contains a multicolored layer called nacre. Sometimes a grain of sand gets inside the shell and the nacre layer begins to build a coating of nacre around the irritating grain, gradually constructing a pearl.

THE MYSTERIOUS PEARL

Muhammad bin Thani, the wise and early leader of the Al-Thani family, once said, "We are all, from the highest to the lowest, slaves of one master, the Pearl." Prior to the 1930s, pearling had been the most important source of income for Qatar for many centuries. Archeological evidence of pearling on the nearby island of Bahrain has been traced back to 3000 B.C. Qatari pearl merchants traded pearls with the Arab Abbasid Empire in Baghdad in the eighth and ninth centuries A.D.

The industry continued to increase in importance until it reached a peak at the time of World War I. The women of Europe and America developed a love affair with the pearl. High fashion demanded necklaces and earrings designed with gleaming pearls. During the peak period of demand, hundreds of dhows sailed from Qatar's coastal villages to anchor over the pearling banks.

The oyster beds, or pearling banks, were found primarily along the western side of the gulf in waters a few miles offshore. The best locations were in the great bay between Qatar and the Musandam Peninsula. One of the favorite spots for pearl divers was the deep water surrounding Halul Island. Divers thought the finest pearls were always found in the deepest water.

The pearling boats left their ports at the beginning of June and normally returned in late September. An average crew was composed of eighteen to twenty members. The captain decided where to anchor the boat and how long to stay in a specific location. He carefully observed the harvesting of the pearl from its shell. Then he negotiated the sale of the pearls and distributed the income to the crew.

Pearling was a very hard life. The heat and humidity were oppressive. The crew was jammed onto the deck of a small boat. They ate fish and rice almost every day for four months. The day began at sunrise with a light breakfast of coffee and dates. The divers entered the water about an hour later and continued to dive until near sunset. Short breaks were taken for prayers and coffee.

The diver had a stone weight attached to his ankle to help carry him to the bottom, sometimes more than 100 feet (30 meters) down. A good diver could stay on the bottom for up to two minutes on his own lung power. He wore nose clips made of turtle shell, and his ears were plugged with wax to prevent the water pressure from rupturing his eardrums. He wore leather caps on his fingers

Natural pearls are sorted by shape, size, and color for sale to jewelry makers the world over. Cultured pearls, invented by the Japanese, put an end to much natural pearling because they could now be produced in consistent sizes.

so that he would not cut them on the oysters' shells. The oysters were picked up and placed in a rope basket. When the diver ran out of air, he tugged on a rope attached to his leg, signaling his partner on deck to pull him to the surface. While the deckhand emptied the basket, the diver relaxed in the water. Within a few minutes, he would plunge back to the bottom again.

Danger was everpresent. Sharks were sometimes attracted to the boats because of the activity of the divers. The most common injury was a severed arm or leg. Occasionally, the smell of blood brought more sharks, and the diver disappeared in a feeding frenzy. Even the bottom wasn't safe. For example, a stonefish looked like a rock on the sea floor. However, if stepped on, or even brushed, the stonefish's sharp spines could be driven into the diver's skin, releasing a deadly poison. In most cases, the diver would die within four days. Jellyfish trailed long threads that looked like nylon. If these brushed a diver's skin, he was burned as if a hot wire had touched him.

With all of the hardships, the discovery of an extraordinarily large pearl brought great joy to the entire crew. Each man would touch the pearl and try to catch the reflection of his face on its surface. It had a hypnotic effect on all who viewed it. A large, high-quality pearl would bring thousands of dollars.

Buyers commissioned by pearl merchants spent the season moving from boat to boat every few days to bid on the pearls that had been found. The pearl merchants then sold the pearls to buyers, who in turn sold them to jewelers all over the world. The dhow crews did all the hard work and made very little money. The merchants and the jewelers became wealthy men.

An economic depression hit America and Europe in the early 1930s. At about the same time, the Japanese introduced cultured pearls. These were real pearls, but they were started in the oysters by humans instead of accident inserting a grain of sand into the oyster. The market in Qatar for natural pearls collapsed. The country suffered a devastating economic blow.

The people in Qatar saw a bleak future. They couldn't know that in less than twenty years, oil would brighten the economic picture more than anyone could dream.

BLACK GOLD

For centuries, Bedouin herded their camels, goats, and sheep across the Jebel Dukhan (meaning "hills of Dukhan"). They were unaware of the riches that lay below the surface. In 1935 Sheikh Abdullah bin Qasim Al-Thani signed an agreement with the Iraq Petroleum Company granting permission to explore for oil and gas. The company discovered oil in 1940. The oil was located in three separate layers. Below the oil was a layer of natural gas. The pool of oil and gas was approximately 35 miles (56 kilometers) long and 8 to 10 miles (13 to 16 kilometers) wide. The pool

Until the middle of the twentieth century, a fortune in petroleum, or "black gold," was hidden under these inconspicuous little hills, called Jebel Dukhan.

contained a very high grade of oil with only a little sulfur.

The first successful well was named Dukhan I. Although World War II slowed the development of the field, by 1949 enough oil was being produced to begin exporting some.

No other major oil deposits were discovered on Qatar's land mass. However, there was growing evidence that pools of oil might exist under the waters of the Persian Gulf within Qatar's territorial limits. In 1952 Shell Petroleum of the Netherlands was given permission to search for offshore oil. During the 1960s, three individual oil fields were found 50 to 60 miles (80 to 96 kilometers) east of Doha in the sparkling gulf waters. Pipelines now carry the oil to Halul Island for storage and export. The storage tanks can hold up to 4.5 million barrels of crude oil. Large supertankers anchor at terminals adjacent to Halul Island and connect to a pipeline that pumps oil into their massive holds. Approximately 90 percent of the total oil production is exported to markets in the Pacific nations of Asia, though some travels to western Europe.

Qatar shares an additional gulf oil field with its neighbor,

This offshore oil platform in the Persian Gulf is owned jointly by Qatar and the neighboring country of Abu Dhabi.

Abu Dhabi. The two neighbors agreed to share ownership and production. A Japanese company supervises the operation.

The production and income from oil increased steadily in the early years. By 1974 production had peaked at 600,000 barrels a day. A major portion of the early profits went to established oil companies owned by foreigners. But the leaders of Qatar believed that the citizens of their country were the rightful owners of their oil. Therefore, they created the Qatar General Petroleum Corporation (QGPC) and negotiated with the foreign oil companies for total ownership of all the oil. For the past twenty years, Qatar has received the full financial benefit of its oil production.

The government has managed the oil resources wisely. They have limited production to 350,000 to 400,000 barrels each day, conserving their reserves. At current rates of production, reserves are expected to last until at least 2005.

The money earned from oil sales has been used to modernize the nation. The pace of change has been watched closely by

Qatar's leaders. They want what is best for their citizens, but they also want to protect the country's rich heritage and traditions from destruction.

INVISIBLE WEALTH

You cannot see it, and you cannot smell it. You cannot hold it in your hand, but you can sell it. It can be the source of great wealth. What is it? A unique fossil fuel called natural gas. Crude oil is liquid petroleum, but natural gas is petroleum in the gaseous state. Sometimes natural gas and crude oil are found in the same pool of petroleum. This gas is called associated gas. At other locations, natural gas is found alone and is called non-associated gas. Qatar has both types of natural gas. In fact, the tiny country of Qatar has larger reserves of natural gas than the entire United States. Qatar's economic future will depend heavily on the development of its natural-gas reserves.

Natural gas is used primarily as a fuel. It can be burned to boil water, which creates steam for generating electricity. It can also be used to power cars and trucks. It burns much cleaner than gasoline and causes less air pollution. Raw materials extracted from natural gas are used to refine crude oil, make fertilizer, and manufacture plastics. Qatar uses its gas for all these functions, primarily at its large industrial complex at Umm Said. Gas from the Dukhan field is transported by pipeline to Umm Said. Associated gas from the three offshore oilfields is also pumped through a pipeline to Umm Said. Recently, a pipeline from the enormous North Field non-associated gas reservoir was tied into the Umm Said Industrial District.

A complex of platforms pumps the natural gas from the giant pool under the Persian Gulf called the North Field, the largest such field in the world and the source of much of Qatar's wealth for the coming decades.

In 1971 a drilling rig operating off the northeast coast of Qatar made a startling discovery. Drilling at a depth of 8,000 to 10,000 feet (2,440 to 3,048 meters) below the floor of the Persian Gulf, the rig hit an immense pocket of non-associated natural gas. It was found to extend from the northeastern tip of the peninsula into the gulf more than 100 miles (161 kilometers). It covered more than 2,000 square miles (5,120 square kilometers), equal to nearly half the total land area of Qatar. Called the North Field, it is the single largest non-associated gas field in the world! It is estimated to contain more than 330 trillion cubic feet (9.3 trillion cubic meters) of recoverable gas.

A spiderweb of pipelines carries crude petroleum from the oil wells of Jebel Dukhan to Umm Said Industrial District, where it is processed.

The development of this major natural resource is the most significant factor in Qatar's economic future. How to develop these massive reserves has become a primary national goal.

Plans were first drafted to begin construction of a gas-processing facility in 1987. The development process was divided into two phases. Phase One was a modest project designed to meet Qatar's domestic gas requirements, especially the nation's growing appetite for electricity and fresh water. The electrical power-generating plants can also be used to convert seawater to fresh water. They use a heat-distilling process known as desalination. In addition, some of the gas was to be used to manufacture natural gas liquids (NGL) for export. Methane, propane, and butane represent the most common natural gas liquids. The remaining gas was earmarked for expanding the industries on the mainland that produce various chemicals from petroleum.

Eight offshore platforms now pump gas to a central location, where it is transported by pipeline to the Umm Said Industrial District. At Umm Said, new processing facilities utilize the gas. Surplus gas is reinjected into a reservoir at Dukhan for future use.

RAS LAFFAN

Phase Two is a much more ambitious project that will extend into the next century. It will cost billions of dollars and involve some foreign investors including Mobil Oil, Total of France, and two Japanese companies. A completely new industrial district is being built at Ras Laffan, approximately 50 miles (80 kilometers) straight north of Doha. The Ras Laffan Industrial Complex will eventually cover 25 square miles (64 square kilometers).

The project was initiated in 1992, when QATARGAS signed an agreement with a Japanese electric-utility company. The Japanese company agreed to purchase 4 million tons of liquefied natural gas (LNG) each year for twenty-five years, starting in 1997. As construction on the project progressed, seven other Japanese utilities signed an agreement to purchase an additional 2 million tons of LNG for twenty-five years. By 2001, a total of 6 million tons of LNG each year will be headed for Japan.

In order to meet the requirements of the Japanese utility companies, QATARGAS engaged in a massive expansion program. Three new drilling platforms with twenty-four separate gas wells were constructed offshore. A 32-inch (81-centimeter) pipeline, 50 miles (80 kilometers) long, was laid on the floor of the gulf to deliver the gas to Ras Laffan. An enormous processing plant was built to convert the gas to a liquid so that it can be transported to

Typical of the major construction being carried out at the Ras Laffan Industrial Complex, where natural gas will be converted to a liquid and shipped abroad, are these scenes of the building of a water-cooling facility.

Japan by special tankers. Liquefaction requires high pressure and extremely low temperatures. Of course, there is no gas pipeline to Japan. Instead, it has to be shipped.

Three towering storage tanks, capable of holding hundreds of thousands of gallons of LNG, were built near the shore next to a new port. Building the new port was a major engineering task. First, a navigation channel from the Persian Gulf to the port had to be dredged. The channel is 3 miles (4.8 kilometers) long, 1,000 feet (300 meters) wide, and 50 feet (15 meters) deep. It connects to a huge harbor that is kept at a depth of 45 feet (14 meters). Billions

The Ras Abu Aboud station near Doha uses natural gas to generate electricity and to convert seawater to drinkable fresh water.

of tons of sand had to be dredged to create the harbor.

A fleet of seven tankers was built in Japan to transport the LNG. The tankers are almost 1,000 feet (300 meters) in length, longer than three football fields. Each tanker costs more than one-quarter of a billion dollars to build. One tanker will carry 4,767,000 cubic feet (135,000 cubic meters) of LNG. Normal cruising speed is 22 miles (35 kilometers) per hour. It takes about one month for a round-trip voyage from Qatar to Japan.

A second stage of Phase Two has Qatar General Petroleum linked with Mobil Oil to produce and export more than 10 million tons of LNG each year. It is predicted that this stage will be completed by the year 2005. The prospective buyers are from South Korea, Taiwan, China, India, Thailand, and Turkey. Several countries in Europe have also expressed an interest in purchasing LNG from Qatar. Soon caravans of tankers full of Qatari LNG will be crossing the world's oceans like camel caravans passing across the graceful dunes of the desert.

INDUSTRY

Electric generation was the first major, modern industry established in Qatar. In 1963, the Ras Abu Aboud power station began generating electricity for Doha, using steam generated by burning natural gas. The small plant has been expanded several times, and new generating plants have been built to increase capacity. In 1977 the Ras Abu Fontas station opened with an electrical generating capacity of 618 megawatts. When the plant started operations, it was the largest gas-fueled plant in the Middle East. Currently, an even larger power station is being built at Al-Wusayl, a few miles north of Doha.

All of Qatar's power-generating stations are located along the Persian Gulf coast because, in Qatar, the power stations serve two purposes. The heat used to create steam to drive the electrical turbines is also used to distill saltwater from the gulf. As the saltwater evaporates, the minerals are left behind and pure water vapor is condensed as fresh water. More than 100 million gallons (378 million liters) of seawater are converted to fresh water each day. In a country that receives only 2 inches (5 centimeters) of rain year, fresh water is a precious resource.

Few factories can survive without the electricity generated by burning natural gas. This is a small textile factory staffed by expatriate workers.

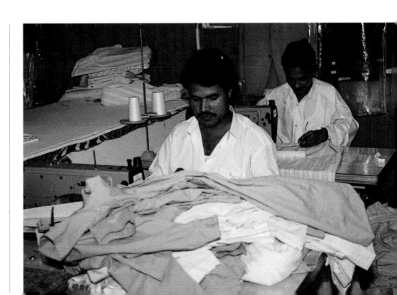

Water towers such as the one at the left are used to store desalinated water, for use in Doha. Rural areas receive their fresh water in trucks, seen above being filled from storage facilities.

Another early Qatari industry is the Qatar National Cement Company, located in a desolate part of western Qatar at Umm Bab. It maintains its own small power and water-desalination plant. Local limestone deposits quarried just a few miles south of the factory serve as the raw material. A recent expansion at the plant increased annual production to 750,000 tons a year.

Most houses are built with concrete blocks covered with a stucco finish. Streets, sewer lines, parking lots, water towers, and reservoirs demand tons of cement. At the current rate of use, the raw materials should last another seventy-five years.

Qatar has long had a major goal of diversifying its industry. The leaders of the country knew that it was dangerous to depend economically on oil and gas alone. With this in mind, they developed the Umm Said Industrial District 25 miles (40 kilometers) south of Doha. The first plant at that location opened in 1968, and it is now

home to almost all of Qatar's heavy industries. However, in the twenty-first century, Ras Laffan Industrial District will likely challenge Umm Said for the leadership role.

Umm Said includes a diversity of industries. The national oil refinery produces a wide range of products including lead-free gasoline and aviation fuel. The refinery meets the national demand for fuel products with some left over for export. A petrochemical company manufactures high-grade ethylene and polyethylene for use in plastics. Two large natural gas liquids (NGL) facilities separate propane, butane, and natural gasoline for export. Finally, Qatar Iron and Steel Company uses a blast furnace and two electric-arc

A cement factory provides concrete blocks for use in building residences (top). The Qatar Fertilizer Company (right) was the first industry to be built in the Umm Said Industrial District.

furnaces to make several different steel products.

In all of the industrial centers, the primary workers are expatriates, people who have chosen to live, work, and raise their families in foreign countries. They come mostly from Pakistan, India, Bangladesh, the Philippines, and Arab countries.

AGRICULTURE

In a country like Qatar, with very little rainfall and not much soil, one might expect that little food is grown. However, the Ministry of Municipal Affairs and Agriculture has done a fine job of encouraging increased food production. The ministry has established experimental farms to improve the quality of livestock and crops. Farmers are provided with low-interest loans to expand and improve their operations. Advice on the use of pesticides and insecticides is also given. Even the latest technology in drip irrigation is made available.

The most successful livestock operation is a large poultry farm a few miles north of Doha. The facility produces both broilers and eggs and meets almost 80 percent of the country's demand. Sheep and goats are still raised in substantial numbers, and lamb remains a favorite meat dish in the Qatari diet. A modest dairy farm produces milk for the local market. Arabian horses are raised for sport, and camels are still popular for a variety of purposes.

The most remarkable advances in agriculture have been in crop production. In 1963 the ministry established the Rawdat al Faras Agricultural Experiment Farm. The farm has served as a model in developing modern techniques in vegetable and fruit production. Most cropland is located in the northern half of Qatar where

Agriculture in Qatar is unlike agriculture in almost any other country. Because there is virtually no natural soil and the air is too dry, both vegetables (above) and flowers (left) are grown in massive greenhouses. Livestock, on the other hand, can be raised by supplying adequate food and fresh water. Below left are sheep and goats that have been brought to a livestock market. Below: Expatriate workers at the Doha Livestock Market are unloading hay for the animals.

Although Qatar is self-sufficient in growing many vegetables, it still has to import some foods, especially fruits. This fine display of produce is in the Doha market.

pockets of soil can be found. Almost two-thirds of the arable land is used to grow vegetables and fruit. The nation is now self-sufficient in winter vegetables and can almost meet its summer vegetable needs.

Greenhouses dot the landscape. Inside the greenhouses, long, firm cucumbers hang on staked plants. Bright red, juicy tomatoes are almost too tempting to pass. Stalks of okra are loaded with pods. As they mature, the greenhouse-grown vegetables are trucked to the large vegetable market in Doha. Alfalfa and other greens are grown to feed livestock.

All the crops require irrigation because there is not enough natural precipitation. The irrigation water is pumped from an aquifer, an underground area of gravel where fresh water collects naturally. The top of an aquifer is called the water table.

Geologists at the University of Qatar have warned farmers that they are using more underground water than they should. If too much water is pumped from the aquifer, space is left for saltwater to creep into it, making all the water useless.

In an attempt to halt the drop in the water table, scientists have launched a new project. In depressions called water fields, rainwater collects after heavy winter downpours. Scientists have worked with engineers to drill into the aquifer above the water table. They install a large pipe with holes in it, like a giant sieve, down into the aquifer. Rainwater that collects in the depression flows into the pipe and recharges the aquifer. In some places, the water table has risen 15 percent since the pipes were installed.

FISHING

The rich waters of the Persian Gulf have attracted fishermen for centuries. Most coastal residents make fish an important part of their diet. In 1980 the Qatar National Fishing Company was organized to provide loans for local fishermen and to operate a fleet of more than three hundred vessels. They also cooperate with other nations around the Persian Gulf to research the waters of the gulf. Recently, concern has been expressed regarding pollution from the petroleum industry and gulf shipping.

There are almost 140 different species of fish commonly found in Qatar's waters. The most popular commercial species is a type of grouper. Fresh fish, as well as shrimp, prawns and crabs, are delivered to the Doha Fish Market daily. In recent years, a growing percentage of the annual catch has been made by Indian and Pakistani fishermen who sail their dhows into Qatar's waters.

Left: This elaborate wedding dress is decorated in pearls.
Above: Qatari businessmen socialize in a coffee house.
Below: This home of a well-to-do Qatari has an Islamic-style entrance.

Chapter 5

THE PEOPLE

Although an accurate census had never been taken before the 1950s, Qatar's population has always been small. Prior to the development of oil in the 1950s, the total population was probably less than 30,000. Today, the population exceeds 500,000 and is growing rapidly. However, probably only about 30 percent of the people who live and work in Qatar are Qatari nationals.

The majority of the people are expatriate workers who were born in foreign countries. They come from Iran, Pakistan, India, the Philippines, Indonesia, and many other countries. These workers are the backbone of the Qatari labor force. They work in the oil fields, industrial plants, and construction. They also perform much of the labor on the farms. Their faces reflect cultures that are distinct from Qatar's, and many languages can be heard in the markets and workplace. One of the major goals of the current government is to replace many foreign workers at management levels in industry with Qatari citizens.

These Iranians have entered Qatar illegally, hoping to sell some of the Persian carpets they brought with them. Most non-Qatari residents are legal expatriates.

The Qatari native population has its roots in tribes from the Arabian Peninsula. The Al-Thani family, with several thousand members, is by far the major family. Almost all native Qataris speak Arabic, follow the teachings of Wahhabi Islam, and reflect the cultural traditions of Arab society.

ISLAM: A WAY OF LIFE

In the life of a Qatari citizen, religion is more important than any other factor. Almost all Qataris are followers of the Wahhabi branch of the Sunni sect of Islam. Most Muslims, as the people who follow the Islamic faith are called, are either Sunni or Shiite, depending on traditions established hundreds of years ago. The Qataris adopted the conservative Wahhabi philosophy of Sunni under their leader, Sheikh Qasim bin Muhammad Al-Thani. Their beliefs are closely tied to those of their neighbors in Saudi Arabia.

Islam is one of the three great religions that developed historically in the Middle East. The first was Judaism, the second Christianity, and the third Islam. All three religions are mono-theistic (with a belief in one god), and all three claim Abraham as the father of their religion. Each religion recognizes Adam and Eve, Noah, Moses, Job, David, and Solomon. The place of worship for Jews is a synagogue, Christians worship in churches or cathedrals, and Muslims worship in mosques. Jews study the Torah and the Old Testament. Christians study the Holy Bible and Muslims study the Holy Qur'an, also known as the Koran.

Islam was founded in the seventh century A.D. by the Prophet Muhammad, who was born in Mecca in Saudi Arabia. Over a long period of time, he received revelations from a being that he

A number of beautiful mosques (Islamic houses of worship) have been built in Qatar. At right is the Omar Ibn al-Khattah Mosque in Doha, seen at night. Above is the Holy Mosque in Al-Khor, on the east coast north of Doha.

identified as the Angel Gabriel. These revelations have been recorded in the Qur'an.

The life of every Qatari is shaped by his or her commitment to the Five Pillars of Islam. The Five Pillars are faith, prayer, concern for the needy, self-purification, and a pilgrimage to Mecca if possible. These make up the framework of a faithful Muslim's life.

The first pillar is the profession of faith, called the *Shahadah.* Several times each day, a Muslim confirms his or her faith in God by stating, "There is no god except Allah, and Muhammad is the messenger of God." To a Muslim, it is important to remember that one must not let money, greed, or power become his or her god.

Writing out pages of the Holy Qur'an in beautiful Arabic script has long been a work of devotion. This page is from an antique copy at the Qatar's Arabian and Islamic Library.

The second pillar of Islam is prayer *(Salat)*. Prayers are offered to God five times each day, at dawn, noon, mid-afternoon, sunset, and nightfall. If possible, a Muslim offers prayers at a mosque. However, if a mosque is not available, a Muslim can pray anywhere; however, one must face the direction of Mecca. A Muslim must clean himself before prayer. Hands, mouth and teeth, nose, face, top of head, neck, ears, arms to the elbows, and feet to the ankle—all must be washed in clean water. On Fridays, a religious leader called the *Imam* gives a sermon at prayer services. In the Muslim world, the weekend begins at noon on Thursday and concludes on Friday, the holy day in the Muslim world.

The third pillar of Islam is *Zakat,* or charity for the needy. Muslims believe that wealth is a gift from God and should be shared with those who are in need. The amount given is between the individual and God. Most Muslims share a minimum of 2.5 percent of their wealth, but many give more.

The fourth pillar of Islam is fasting *(Siyam)*. All healthy adult Muslims are expected to fast during the month of Ramadan. The fast requires that adults abstain from food, drink, and sex from dawn until sunset each day during that month. It is believed that a person who fasts will have sympathy for those who go hungry. Children, the sick, the elderly, and pregnant women are excused

Because depicting the human figure in art is against Islamic code, the art of beautiful lettering, or calligraphy, has long been important. This man is demonstrating calligraphy at the University of Qatar.

from fasting during Ramadan, but they can make up the fasting days later in the year.

The fifth and final pillar of Islam is the pilgrimage *(Hajj)*. All Muslims are required to participate in the Hajj at least once in their life if they are physically and financially able. The Hajj is an annual pilgrimage to Mecca, in Saudi Arabia, to worship at the Ka'bah. Muslims believe the Ka'bah was a temple originally built by Abraham. The pilgrims also walk seven times between the mountains of Safa and Marwa, then they join in prayer on the wide plain of Arafa. The Hajj ends with a festival called Eid al-Adha. This festival is celebrated with prayers and exchanging of gifts, much like Christmas for Christians. This is an exciting time of the year for Muslim children all over the world, not just for those participating in Hajj.

THE FAMILY

The role of the family in Qatar's society is very important. The family is a source of strength. Parents are treated with great respect by their children. Elders are held in high esteem. When an elderly person enters a room, everyone stands to show respect. Children are trained to behave and not be disrespectful, in any fashion, to their parents or other adults. While some women enter the work force, most mothers with small children commit their lives to raising their children.

Families do many things together. They go to the beach to picnic and swim. They travel to the desert to camp and to dig for tasty truffles (special fungi that grow underground) when they are in season. Fathers spend time with their sons, teaching them how to play soccer and encouraging them in their religious training. Mothers and daughters go to the markets together and look for clothes, jewelry, perfume, and shoes. Families also enjoy eating out at popular Western-style restaurants such as Dairy Queen, Pizza Hut, and Popeye's Fried Chicken. Many residents of Doha spend evenings walking with friends along the Corniche, the modern thoroughfare along the bay.

Most women in Qatar wear the traditional *abaya* and *shayla* (robe and scarf), though very few cover their faces with the *burqa* (veil). Special occasions are marked by decorating a woman's hands and feet with henna, a red dye. Wafting of incense is a tradition of circulating the smoke from burning incense burners under one's clothing.

People in trouble or despair always turn to their families. The family discusses what schools children should attend and helps

Some women leave the home to teach, such as this professor (above) in the women's division of the University of Qatar. She wears a traditional robe and scarf. Some women lead their lives in the seclusion of the strict Muslim, leaving home only in full veil (right). Qatari children have plenty of places to play (below) before starting school.

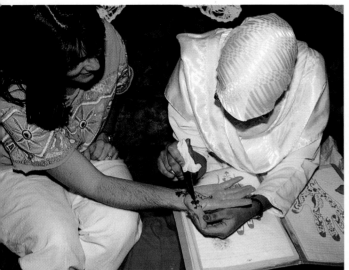

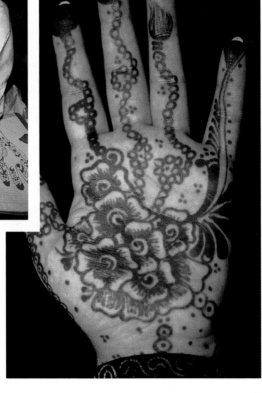

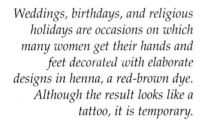

Weddings, birthdays, and religious holidays are occasions on which many women get their hands and feet decorated with elaborate designs in henna, a red-brown dye. Although the result looks like a tattoo, it is temporary.

young men and women decide who is the right person to marry. When parents get older, their children care for them. There are no nursing homes in Qatar. The Qatari people do not feel that it is a difficult task to take care of their parents. Believing it is a privilege to care for their elderly parents, they frequently take them into their own homes when they can no longer care for themselves.

HOSPITALITY

Visitors to Qatar are impressed with the friendliness and warmth with which they are received. An invitation to dinner in a Qatari home is a special honor. One of the customs in Arab society

Special occasions may also bring out the traditional jewelry of a young Qatari woman.

involves the generosity of the host. Food is always prepared in quantities that are much larger than a guest can possibly eat. It would be a disaster for the host if his guest desired more food and there was none left. Sometimes food is served in the traditional manner with guests seated on the floor eating with their hands.

Before the meal, coffee or tea is usually served. The Arabica coffee is brewed in brass coffee pots with the spice called cardamom, which gives it a distinct aroma and flavor. It is served in small procelain cups. Guests normally drink three to five cups. When they have had enough, they hold the cup in an outstretched arm and wiggle their wrist back and forth to signal to their host that they do not desire any more coffee. Hot tea laced with mint and sugar may be served in small glass mugs. Coffee and tea are offered at business meetings as well as at home.

In the afternoons and evenings, male visitors are invited to coffee houses to drink coffee, smoke, and engage in lively conversation. Some men smoke tobacco, while others smoke

Doha offers families a chance to enjoy such Western restaurants as a Dairy Queen (above), but hospitality in the home requires a more traditional offering of coffee, usually served in a classic Arabic coffee pot (right).

fermented fruit in a water pipe called the hubble-bubble. The conversation usually turns to politics, economics, or religion. Arabs enjoy the art of conversation.

URBAN LIFE

Today, almost all Qataris live in rebuilt villages or cities. Doha, the capital city, is a thriving metropolis of more than 250,000 residents, more than half the population of the country. The city has been transformed from a mud-hut village with dirt pathways into a gleaming city by the bay.

Doha wraps around a large bay that reflects the modern architecture of an active commercial and governmental center. The Corniche, a six-lane divided thoroughfare, follows the curve of the bay for 5 miles (8 kilometers) from the airport to the dazzling Sheraton Doha Hotel. The Sheraton Doha is designed like a pyramid and is one of many fine, five-star, international hotels. The government ministry buildings are stunning architectural masterpieces lining the Corniche. Streets join the Corniche at intersections called roundabouts. The center of each roundabout contains gardens and very unusual large sculptures of such items as rosewater pitchers, coffee urns, oyster shells with pearls, and clocktowers. Horns honk and drivers shake their fists as cars merge into the heartbeat of traffic that flows along the Corniche.

In the center of all of this, the Emiri Palace (the *Diwan*) stands on a slight hill overlooking the bay. Here, the emir, Sheikh Hamad bin Khalifah Al-Thani, conducts the business of government. All citizens have the right to call on the emir at the palace and discuss issues with him. As a matter of fact, his phone number is listed in the telephone book! One day the emir may visit with a simple Bedouin and the next day he may be in complex discussions with the leaders of another country.

One of the most interesting sections of Doha is the old market, called the *souq.* Shoppers enter a main gate and immediately find themselves in a maze of narrow alleys that wind through a complex network of shops. Iranian merchants bargain over barrels of fresh-roasted cashews and almonds. A tanned, weather-worn face smiles and invites the shopper to smell the herbal teas and home-cure medicines. The aroma of incense and perfume has an intoxicating effect on the visitor. Gold shops with elaborate

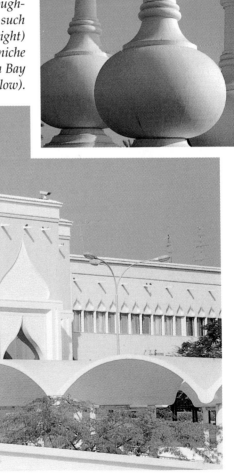

The Corniche (above) is a major thoroughfare that circles Doha Bay. Sculptures such
as these giant rosewater bottles (right)
make walking or riding along the Corniche
a delight. On a hill overlooking Doha Bay
is the Diwan, or Emiri Palace (below).

The Sheraton Doha Hotel is a stunning pyramid that is reflected in the waters of Doha Bay. Its design is based on the Mayan pyramids of Central America.

necklaces and other jewelry dot the narrow aisles. The melodic chant of the call to prayer floats across the souq as merchants close their shops for a few minutes of devotion.

ARTS

Music, poetry, and dancing are traditions that reach back thousands of years into Qatar's past. Music was one of the methods that sailors and pearl divers used to break the monotony of many months at sea. Some pearling boats had a singer who used his voice to lift the spirits of the crew. His songs reminded the men to be patient and to remember their loved ones at home. Sometimes the men joined in song with him and other times they clapped their hands in rhythm to the music.

In the desert, the Bedouin were noted for their poetry and storytelling skills. Even today in Qatar, the art of storytelling is still respected. The story often has a moral such as loyalty, strength, compassion, or honor.

These musicians are accompanying the Al-Ardah, a traditional dance performed by men at feasts and national celebrations.

Traditional dances are still performed in the same manner as they have been for centuries. The Al-Ardah dance has one version for the sea and another for the desert. Musicians accompany the dancers with drums, pipes, flutes, tambourines, and stringed instruments. The dancers form two lines facing each other and sway to the rhythm of the music. On many occasions, the men dance with swords to depict battles in the desert. Dancing is frequently performed at weddings, holidays, and civic events.

One of the most remarkable patrons of the arts in Qatar is Sheikh Hassan bin Muhammad bin Ali Al-Thani. Even before he turned thirty years of age, young Sheikh Hassan was devoted his life to preserving the history of Qatar and Arab society. His first project was a museum to display Islamic weapons. It has been recognized as the finest Islamic weapons collection in the world. Next, he established an Arabian and Islamic Library. The library includes a rare collection of Qur'ans dating to the ninth century

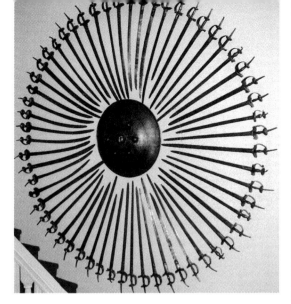

Above: An exhibit of Islamic blades was collected by a young sheikh. Right: This antique chest, now in a museum, would have been a useful piece of furniture in a Qatari home, but it is also a work of art.

A.D. There is also a copy of the first book printed in the Arab world. The book is a Holy Bible printed in Aleppo, Syria, in 1706. Sheikh Hassan's third project is an art museum featuring Arab artists, including some highly skilled artists from Qatar.

Perhaps the best-known museum in Qatar is the Qatar National Museum. New buildings have been carefully designed to blend into the architecture of an old palace. The palace originally belonged to Sheikh Abdullah bin Qasim Al-Thani, who ruled Qatar from 1913 to 1949. Traditional furniture, clothing, and housewares are displayed as a reflection of earlier times. The museum also displays a Bedouin tent and the necessities of life in the desert. Archeological pieces from thousands of years in the past are displayed in a special section of the museum, which also includes a lagoon with dhows and an aquarium exhibit.

This young bird is being trained by a Qatari falconer. Bred especially for their hunting skills, such birds have been used for royal hunting in the Middle East for thousands of years.

SPORTS

The people of Qatar love to watch and participate in sports activities. There are many fine clubs where members can swim, play football (soccer), basketball, volleyball, and other sports. Physical fitness is encouraged for all citizens. Sports activities in Qatar are segregated by the sexes. Boys of all ages participate in youth sports leagues. Girls are more likely to swim, jog, and engage in aerobics.

The most popular sport in the country is soccer. Qatar's National Soccer Team has been very competitive in international matches. Tennis has been growing in popularity. The nation

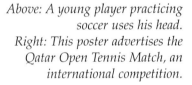

Above: A young player practicing soccer uses his head.
Right: This poster advertises the Qatar Open Tennis Match, an international competition.

sponsors the Qatar Open Tennis Match. The top tennis players in the world compete for hundreds of thousands of dollars in prize money at the Khalifah International Tennis Complex in Doha.

Horses are very popular in Qatar. The Prophet Muhammad encouraged every Muslim to care for a horse if possible. The Arabian horse is highly valued the world over for its strength, beauty, and nobility. Horse-racing, equestrian shows, and jumping competitions draw large crowds. In 1995 the first annual Desert Marathon was held, drawing riders from all over the world, including American movie star Patrick Swayze. One of the best

The Arabian horse is known worldwide for its strength, beauty, and nobility. In Qatar, devotees of the breed belong to the Qatar Racing and Equestrian Club (above). Show horses (right) are given great care and training.

stables in the country is owned by the emir, Sheikh Hamad bin Khalifah Al-Thani. One of his horses was named 1994 World Champion Mare at the Paris Horse Show.

Qatar's most unusual sport is camel racing. While Islam does not allow betting on the races, it is permissible to give luxurious prizes to the winners. The owner of a winning camel might receive a new Mercedes Benz, for example. Some of the top racing camels sell for as much as $3 million. The length of the race is 5 to 7 miles

(8 to 10 kilometers). The jockeys are young boys who wear pants with Velcro bottoms that hold them to the saddles, which also have Velcro patches. Once the boy mounts the saddle, the Velcro keeps him from falling off during a very rough ride. The owners drive alongside the camels during the race, separated by a steel railing. They shout and honk their horns, encouraging their camels and jockeys. It is one of the wildest scenes in the sporting world.

Young boys (right) train as camel jockeys. They get a very rough but special ride, hanging on tightly when their racing camel is running at full stride (below).

Above: Qatar hosted an Olympics sponsored by the Gulf Cooperation Council for its member nations.
Below: The General Post Office in Doha is the largest postal complex in the Middle East.

Chapter 6

CONNECTIONS
TO THE FUTURE

TRANSPORTATION

As a nation whose life focused on the sea, Qatar has long had port facilities. However, as Qatar's economy has grown, these facilities have been expanded to meet the needs of international shipping. Doha Port handles general trade items such as machinery, food, paper goods, transportation equipment and electronic supplies. The port can handle nine medium to large ships at a time. It also has facilities to handle significant numbers of the small dhows that scurry back and forth across the Persian Gulf to Iran, India, Pakistan, and other Arab nations.

Umm Said Harbor is an industrial port. It is the key facility for Qatar's exports. Petroleum, natural gas liquids, fertilizer, and petrochemicals leave the port destined for markets primarily in Asia and other Arab states. In the twenty-first century, the new port at Ras Laffan will begin to overtake Umm Said for the dominant role in Qatar's exports.

Qatar is served by an excellent international airport facility in Doha. The airport is equipped to handle all types of aircraft including the largest jumbo jets. A 15,000-foot (4,545-meter)

A Doha television camera crew films events of importance in Qatar. This crew is broadcasting the Gulf Cooperation Council Olympics.

runway assures safe landing conditions for planes arriving from all over the world. The Doha International Airport is convenient, only 2 miles (3.2 kilometers) from Doha's city center. This allows visitors quick and easy access to government offices, banking services, energy companies, and a number of first-class hotels.

Gulf Air is the national airline of Qatar. This airline is owned equally by Qatar, Bahrain, Oman, and the United Arab Emirates. In recent years, Gulf Air has begun to fly to more cities around the world. The company flies modern airplanes with highly trained pilots and crews. It has established a reputation for five-star service, even earning several awards for the superb quality of its international food service.

In order to meet the growing need for aviation specialists, Gulf Air established the Civil Aviation College in Doha. It is used for training citizens from the four ownership countries. These students enroll in courses in air traffic control, electronic equipment maintenance, meteorology, and aviation services. Recently, the college introduced a pilot-training program.

The highway system in Qatar focuses on the city of Doha like the spokes of a wheel. Four-lane superhighways radiate to the north, south, and west from Doha, connecting all major regions. The road to Salwa connects with the Saudi Arabian highway network, providing access to the Mediterranean. Another link ties into the transportation system in Abu Dhabi, which connects to the countries of the Lower Gulf. Many of the highways stretch across vast expanses of uninhabited desert. The Qataris love to drive fast. Because there is no speed limit, their Mercedes and BMWs are often a blur, driven at speeds in excess of 100 miles (167 kilometers) per hour.

One of the most popular pastimes in Qatar is off-road driving. Large areas of sand dunes stretch along the east coast from Umm Said to Khor al-Udaid. On weekends, the dunes are dotted with an assortment of four-wheel-drive vehicles and dune buggies. The urban dwellers love to go to the desert. However, the ecology of the desert is very fragile, and environmentalists are beginning to be concerned about potential damage.

COMMUNICATIONS

The postal service in Qatar uses the most modern technology in the world to provide efficient service. The General Post Office in Doha is the largest complex in the Middle East. Its automatic mail-sorting machines can process thousands of letters each hour. More than 25,000 computerized post office boxes are available for residents and businesses. Twenty-eight additional post offices are

The Earth Station for Satellite Communications keeps Qatar in communication with the world.

located in the capital and other cities. Three to four times each year, the Qatar General Post Office designs, prints, and issues beautiful commemorative stamps that are eagerly bought by collectors around the world.

The Qatar Public Telecommunications Corporation provides the very latest technology in telephone service. Telephone, cable, telex, and fax services can be exchanged with any part of the world. Businessmen carry pagers that alert them to important messages. A U.S. company, Motorola, has introduced mobile telephone service, with reception and transmission stations throughout Qatar. The cellular phone has become one of the most popular means of communication.

On the highway from Doha to Dukhan, giant satellite dishes suddenly rise above the bleak landscape. The Earth Station for Satellite Communications has three giant dishes as well as several towers. The Doha 1 dish was constructed in 1971 and draws its television signals from a satellite positioned over the Indian Ocean. Doha 2, an even larger dish, was completed in 1985 to provide programs from the United States, Canada, Latin America, and Europe via an Atlantic Ocean satellite. Finally, in 1986, the Qatar 1 dish linked the country with the Arab world through the

An ambassador from Oman arrives for a meeting of the Gulf Cooperation Council.

Arabsat satellite. Qatari citizens especially enjoy police stories, action movies, and documentaries such as National Geographic Society specials.

A PLACE IN THE WORLD

Since declaring its independence on September 3, 1971, Qatar has rapidly assumed a position of respect in world affairs. A few days after becoming independent, Qatar joined the United Nations and the League of Arab States. The country has maintained an active role in both organizations. Qatar has been generous in its foreign aid programs. Frequently, it donates a large portion of its national income, often more than any other independent state, for support of underdeveloped countries.

Qatar has established diplomatic relations with most major world governments. Its representatives have participated regularly at meetings of the United Nations General Assembly. The leaders of the nation believe strongly in referring political disagreements to this international body. That is why they have requested that the International Court of Justice help resolve their dispute with Bahrain over ownership of the Hawar Islands.

The emir of the time, shown under a portrait of himself, spoke in 1976 at the meeting of the OPEC ministers, when the world was reacting to raised oil prices.

The State of Qatar has played a very important role in the Gulf Cooperation Council (GCC). Established in 1981, the GCC is made up of Qatar, Saudi Arabia, Kuwait, Oman, Bahrain, and the United Arab Emirates. Their goal is to promote political cooperation, to coordinate military and defense issues, and to promote economic growth among the members. Trade agreements, joint military exercises, and political resolutions have been an active part of the GCC programs.

As a member of the GCC, Qatar took a strong stand against Iraq's invasion of Kuwait in 1990. The leaders denounced the invasion and provided troops in the Desert Storm military action that liberated Kuwait. They also have been vocal critics of Israeli occupation of Arab territories. At the same time, they have worked quietly in promoting the peace process between Israelis and Arabs. Qatar was the first GCC country to invite the Israeli foreign minister to participate in talks regarding peace and to encourage possible economic ties.

Membership in the GCC has also meant that Qatar has given full support to halt the suffering of the Somali people. Qataris donated generous relief assistance to Somalia. They have also been outspoken in their criticism of the brutal treatment of the Muslim residents of Bosnia-Herzegovina.

As an oil-producing country, Qatar has been a full member of the Organization of Petroleum Exporting Countries (OPEC) since 1971. In the international picture, Qatar is not one of the giant producers. Oil production is modest, at about 350,000 to 400,000 barrels per day. However, Qatar has always maintained a strong position within the organization. It joined in the now famous Arab Oil Embargo in 1973, which had a significant impact on American energy policy. The country has been a voice of moderation in OPEC, calling for production policies that encourage stability in both prices and supplies. Qatar's role in OPEC may decline as oil reserves are depleted in the early part of the twenty-first century. That does not mean that Qatar will decline as a significant player in the world energy picture. As a matter of fact, the sun is now rising on a new energy future—natural gas.

QATAR'S FUTURE

Few countries have as bright a future as Qatar. Its political leaders have been cautious in measuring development by the impact it will have on the traditional culture. The country has wisely invested its income in providing first-class education, health care, housing, utilities, and a wide range of other services for its citizens. Plans are being developed to diversify the economy and to replace some foreign workers with Qatari nationals. The progress will be fueled by revenue from the enormous North Field natural-gas reserves. Qatar is a nation on the move!

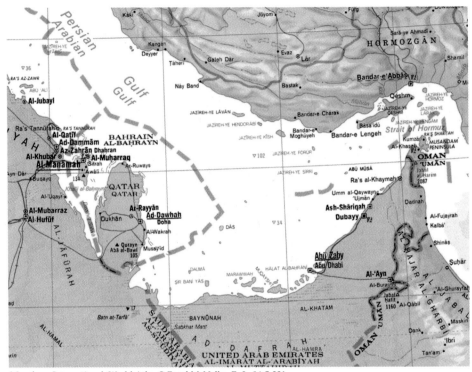

Map from International World Atlas © Rand McNally, R. L. 96-S-221

Close-up of the Qatar region of the Persian Gulf

MINI-FACTS AT A GLANCE

GENERAL INFORMATION

Official Name: Dawlat Qatar (State of Qatar).

Capital: Doha

Government: Absolute monarchy (emirate). Legislation is based on Islamic laws. The *emir* is the head of the state and of government, and possesses supreme power. The Basic Law of 1970 declared Qatar a sovereign and independent state, and established *Shar'ia* (Islamic Law) as the principal source of legislation, dealing essentially with family and personal matters. Secular courts hear civil and criminal cases. It also provides for the formation of a State Advisory Council or *Majlis a'Shura*. The majority of the government officials are members of the royal family. There are no legislature or political parties. For administrative purposes, the country is divided into nine municipalities.

Religion: The official religion is Islam. Most Qataris are Wahhabi Muslims.

Ethnic Composition: Some 30 percent of the population is made up of Qatari nationals; about 70 percent of the people are foreign workers, or expatriates. Most of the foreign workers are from India, Pakistan, Iran, the Philippines, Indonesia, Bangladesh, and Sri Lanka.

Language: Arabic is the official language. English is used for business purposes, and the majority of Qataris understand it.

National Flag: The original Qatari flag was red. In 1949 the red color was changed to maroon. The white serrated band on the hoist side was added later. The nine white points between the maroon and white are decorative and have no special meaning.

National Emblem: The emblem consists of a local sailing boat flanked by two crossed swords within a circle. The circle is white at the top and maroon at the bottom. Qatar's name in Arabic appears on the white portion.

National Anthem: The Qatari national anthem consists of a tune without words.

National Calendar: Gregorian and an Islamic lunar calendar.

Money: The Qatar riyal of 100 dirham is the official currency. In October 1996, 3.63 QR were worth one US dollar.

Membership in International Organizations: Arab Bank for Economic Development in Africa (ABEDA); Arab Fund for Economic and Social

Development (AFESD); Arab League (AL); Arab Monetary Fund (AMF); General Agreement on Tariffs and Trade (GATT); Islamic Development Bank (IDB); Organization of Arab Petroleum Exporting Countries (OAPEC); Organization of Petroleum Exporting Countries (OPEC); United Nations (UN).

Weights and Measures: The metric system is in use.

Population: 1996 population estimates 500,000, with 18 persons per sq. mi. (45 persons per sq. km); about 90 percent live in cities, the remainder in rural areas.

Cities:

Doha 236,131
Ar-Rayyan 99,939
Al-Wakrah 25,747
Umm Said 12,111
(Based on 1987 population estimates.)

GEOGRAPHY

Border: The only land boundary is with Saudi Arabia and the United Arab Emirates in the south. The Persian Gulf makes the western, northern, and eastern boundaries.

Coastline: About 350 mi. (563 km)

Land: The small country of Qatar is located just one degree north of the Tropic of Cancer, along the western coast of the Persian Gulf. Composed mostly of sandstone and limestone, the Qatar Peninsula is covered with sand, gravel, and cobble-size stones. Windblown sand and sand dunes cover most of the south. Elevation gradually increases from east to west, ending in a range of hills, Jebel Dukhan, parallel to the west coast. Qatar's major oil field lies beneath this range of hills. In the north-central part, rainwater collects in depressions in winter, creating the most important agricultural areas of Qatar.

Qatar has jurisdiction over several islands, such as Ra's Rakan in the north, Qarradh and Umm Tais in the west, and the Hawar Archipelago in the south. The Hawar Islands, located about 1.5 mi. (2.3 km) from mainland Qatar and 15 mi. (23 km) from Bahrain, are claimed by both Bahrain and Qatar.

Highest Point: Jebel Dukhan, 250 ft. (75 m)

Lowest Point: At sea level

Rivers: Qatar has very little natural water. There are a few small seasonal rivers (*wadis*) that dry up in the summer months. The groundwater has an extremely high mineral content and is used only for agriculture.

Forests: Natural vegetation is very sparse, and is totally absent in large tracts. Sandy and stony deserts cannot support much plant life. Still, some 130 different plant species thrive in Qatar; they bloom briefly during December to February when the rain falls. During the rains, desert grasses and shrubs provide rich grazing for goats, sheep, and camels.

Wildlife: Wildlife is limited to desert rats, toads, lizards, gazelles, hedgehogs, snakes, and turtles. Two wildlife reserves breed gazelles in captivity, and some private estates breed the white Arabian oryx. Thousands of migratory birds, including flamingos and cormorants, feed in the shallow waters of the Khor al-Udaid Bay in the south. Shra'ouh Island is noted as a resting place for birds.

Climate: Qatar's climate is very hot. The summers are the warmest, with daytime temperatures reaching 104° F. (40° C) regularly. Average winter temperatures are 50° to 60°F. (10° to 20° C). The *shamal* is a very unpleasant hot wind that blows from the north. Dust storms and sandstorms are common. Humidity is very high (about 90 percent) along the coastal region. Rainfall is extremely rare. Qatar receives less than 2 inches (5 cm) of annual rainfall, mostly concentrated in the winter month of December.

Greatest Distance: North to South: 125 mi. (201 km).
                           East to West: 55 mi. (88 km).

Area: 4,247 sq. mi. (11,437 sq. km).

ECONOMY AND INDUSTRY

Agriculture: Less than 1 percent of the land is under cultivation, and almost all cultivation is dependent on irrigation. Almost two-thirds of the arable land is used to grow vegetables and fruit, such as cucumbers, tomatoes, melons, and okra. Alfalfa is grown as a feed crop; some wheat and barley are also grown, but most of the basic food items are imported. Land is owned by the government. The government operates experimental farms to improve the quality of livestock and crops, such as cereals, vegetables, and dates. With help from drip irrigation, farming of vegetables is becoming more popular.

A large poultry farm operates near Doha providing eggs and chickens for local consumption. Sheep and lamb are raised primarily for food. Arabian horses are raised for sports. The camel is still a popular possession for Qatari families. The most popular commercial fish is a type of grouper; other varieties of seafood include shrimp, prawns, and crabs.

Mining: Qatar produces about 1 percent of the total oil production of the world. Halul Island is the major oil-storage center and port for shipping Qatar's oil and gas. Pipelines carry oil to Halul Island for storage and export. Qatar also shares an offshore oil field with neighboring Abu Dhabi of the United Arab Emirates. The government has managed oil reserves wisely and has limited production to 350,000 to 400,000 barrels a day. At this rate of production, Qatari oil will last for several years into the twenty-first century. Some 90 percent of oil is exported to other countries. Qatar is very rich in natural gas. Qatar's enormous North Field gas reservoir is the single largest gas field in the world, with more than 330 trillion cubic feet (9.3 trillion cubic meters) of recoverable reserves.

Manufacturing: Dhows, the traditional boats, have been made in Qatar for centuries. Even today, the skilled craftsmen of the boatyards of Doha construct dhows without any plans or drawings; they measure wood planks with experienced eyes only. Electricity-generating and desalination plants make electricity and in the same process convert seawater to fresh water; more than 100 million gallons (378 million liters) of seawater are converted to fresh water every day in Qatar. Petroleum refining, fertilizer manufacturing, and plastics are the major industries. The large Umm Said Industrial Complex has petroleum, natural gas, and related industries. Another industrial complex is being built with the investment of billions of dollars at Ras Laffan. The Qatar National Cement Company is located at Umm Bab, in western Qatar. Small-scale industries include food-processing, textiles, furniture, and paper.

Transportation: There are no railroads in Qatar. In the early 1990s, some 670 miles (1,080 kilometers) of roads connected all major towns. These roads are fairly new and in excellent condition; there is no speed limit, and people some-times drive more than 100 miles (160 km) per hour. Modern automobiles and four-wheel-drive trucks are the most common means of transportation. Four-lane highways connect Doha with other major towns, including towns in Saudi Arabia. In Doha, a beautiful six-lane divided road, called the Corniche, follows the curve of Doha Bay for 5 miles (8 km), and is decorated with elaborate sculptures of rosewater containers, coffee urns, and oyster shells with pearls. Doha is the chief seaport and has an international airport. Gulf Air, the national airline, is equally owned by Qatar, Bahrain, Oman, and the United Arab Emirates. Doha port handles trade items such as machinery, food, paper goods, transportation equipment, and electronic supplies. The Umm Said port exports petroleum, natural gas, fertilizer, and petrochemicals.

Communication: Qatar has four daily newspapers with a total circulation of about 70,000. Most of the newspapers are in Arabic, but English papers are also available. The main post office complex is the largest of its kind in the Middle East. Qatari stamps are collected all over the world for their beautiful designs. Qatar has developed as an important center for banking and trade in the Persian Gulf region, and is well connected by the latest telecommunications technology with the business centers of the world. Cellular phones, pagers, telex, and faxes are very popular and are commonly used. In the early 1990s, there was one radio receiver for every three persons, one television set for 2.5 persons, and one telephone for five persons.

Trade: Qatar has had a favorable trade balance for several years — its export amount is almost double its import amount. Chief imports are machinery and transportation equipment, manufactured goods, food and live animals, and chemicals and chemical products. Major import sources are Japan, the United States, United Kingdom, Germany, Italy, France, United Arab Emirates, and Saudi Arabia. Chief export items are crude petroleum, petroleum products, and liquefied gas. Major export destinations are Japan, Thailand, Singapore, South Korea, United Arab Emirates, Italy, India, and Saudi Arabia.

EVERYDAY LIFE

Health: Health-care facilities are good in Qatar. The government provides free medical care to all, including foreign workers. Primary health-care centers operate in every town; serious cases are referred to the main hospital in Doha. The Hamad Medical Corporation in Doha has three separate hospitals. A hospital for women is staffed by women doctors and nurses. Life expectancy, at 71 years for males and 76 years for females, places Qatar on a par with Western industrial nations. In the early 1990s, there was one physician per 670 persons and one hospital bed per 480 persons. The infant-mortality rate is low—13 per 1,000.

Education: Education is not compulsory, but more than 98 percent of school-age children attend schools. Education from the first grade to university level is completely free of tuition. Primary education starts at six years of age and continues for six years; it is followed by three years of preparatory school and then three years of secondary school. Children are taught math, language, science, religion, and social studies. Following Islamic law, schools are segregated for boys and girls. Children of foreign workers go to private schools where coeducation is allowed. The University of Qatar is the only institution of higher learning. More girls than boys enroll in the higher educational institutes. An aviation training college is at Doha. Religious schools teach the Holy Qur'an to young boys. The government runs special programs to promote adult literacy. In the early 1990s, the literacy rate was about 75 percent, one of the highest in the Middle East.

Holidays:
National Day, September 30

Islamic holidays such as the beginning of Ramadan, Id al-Fib, Id al-Adha, Islamic New Year, and Leilat al-Meiraj are based on the Islamic lunar calendar and differ by a day or two every year.

Culture: Qatar is one of the richest nations in the world, with a high per capita income. The oil money has been wisely used by the ruling emirs to modernize the nation. The Museum of Islamic Weapons has one of the finest collections of those weapons. The Arabian and Islamic Library has a rare collection of Holy Qur'ans. The Qatar National Museum houses traditional furniture, clothing, tents, dhows, and housewares. Music, poetry, and dancing have been part of the Qatar culture for centuries. The art of storytelling is well respected. Dancing is frequently performed at weddings, holidays, and civic events. Only men take part in dancing; sometimes they dance with swords to depict battles in the desert. Some modern buildings are architectural masterpieces. The Sheraton Doha Hotel is designed like a pyramid. The Emiri Palace (the *Diwan*) is located on a slight hill overlooking the bay. The older section of Doha is congested, with houses and shops on both sides of the narrow streets. The old market *(souq)* is a maze of narrow alleys winding through a complex network of small shops.

Society: Religion is the most important factor in Qatari life. Children are taught to have great respect for their elders. The family is the center of all Qatari social events, and the source of strength for its members. Male dominance has always existed at all age levels in Qatari society. The father provides for the family and the mother runs the household and takes care of the children. Older parents live with, and are taken care of, by the extended families.

Marriages are arranged by parents and grandparents. Recently more and more women have been joining the work force as teachers, journalists, and medical professionals. Qatari society has very little crime; drug and alcohol abuse are almost nonexistent, as these crimes have severe punishments. Traditional Qatari society was previously based on nomadic grazing, fishing, pearling, and off-shore trade. The camel, called the "ship of the desert," was an important feature in nomadic Qatari society; it provided milk, meat, hair (for cloth, slippers, and tent), and skin for making bags to carry water.

Dress: Traditionally, Qatari men wear a white flowing robe, *thobe,* and a head-dress, *gutra,* that is secured by a braided cloth ring. Most women wear a black robe, *abaya,* and a scarf, *hijab.* People tend to wear loose-fitting clothing that allows air to circulate around the body. Cotton garments are the most popular as they absorb moisture. On special occasions, women decorate their hands and feet with henna, a reddish-brown dye.

Housing: The government has been very generous with housing for Qatari residents. Houses are provided, complete with furniture, to poorer Qatari citizens. Modern houses are one or two stories high with three or four bedrooms, laundry, storage, and garages. Most newer houses are built with concrete blocks and are covered with a stucco finish. Apartment buildings have been built in Doha and other industrial centers for foreign workers and their families.

Food: Lamb is the favorite meat dish in the Qatari diet, along with chicken, rice, wheat bread, and vegetables. Muslims do not eat pork. *Felafel* (beans with olive oil and garlic) is served with pita bread. Another popular dish is *sheesh kebob* — chunks of meat roasted on a skewer with vegetables. Traditionally, food is eaten sitting on the floor and with the right hand. Recently, Western-style fast-food places such as Dairy Queen, Pizza Hut, and Popeye's Fried Chicken have become popular in Doha. Distilled seawater provides more than half of the drinking water in Qatar. Coffee and tea are the most popular beverages; Islam forbids consumption of alcohol. Some men smoke fermented fruit and tobacco in a water pipe called the hubble-bubble.

Sports and Recreation: Falconry is an age-old traditional sport. Soccer is the favorite sport, followed by tennis. Sports clubs (separate for boys and girls) are popular where children play soccer, basketball, volleyball, and other team sports. The Khalifah International Tennis Complex is at Doha. Horse- and camel-racing draw big cheering crowds. The Arabian horse is highly valued for its strength, beauty, and nobility. Recreation activities center around the family. Men spend hours at the roadside coffee houses, and women socialize at home.

Social Welfare: Qatar's social welfare system, funded by the oil revenues, is designed to take care of the needy citizens from birth to death. Free medical care is available to everyone residing in Qatar. The government pays a fixed amount of money to widows, orphans, and elderly people. Older and sick relatives are taken care of by the family members.

IMPORTANT DATES

3,000 B.C. — Records of pearl diving in Qatar exist.

323 B.C. — Records show that an admiral of Alexander the Great visits Qatar.

1766 — The Al-Khalifahs settle at Zubarah, in northwest Qatar.

1783 — Sheikh Ahmed bin Mohammad ibn Khalifah becomes the ruler of Bahrain.

1795 — Qatar is conquered by Saudi Arabia and the Wahhabis.

1821 — The British bombard Doha as punishment for an alleged act of piracy.

1867 — The Al-Thani family refuses to pay tribute to Bahrain; Bahrain and Abu Dhabi attack Doha and Al-Wakrah, almost wiping them out of existence.

1871 — The Ottoman Turks demand that Qatar acknowledge Turkish supremacy and fly the Turkish flag.

1878 — Sheikh Qasim attacks Zubarah and eliminates Bahrain's presence from the northwestern coast.

1893 — The Ottoman Turks attack Doha; Sheikh Qasim's forces defeat the Turks.

1916 — Sheikh Abdullah signs an agreement of peace with the British; Qatar becomes a protectorate of Great Britain.

1935 — Sheikh Abdullah signs an agreement with the Iraq Petroleum Company that permits oil and gas exploration in Qatar.

1939 — Great Britain grants Hawar Islands to Bahrain; an appeal is still pending before the International Court of Justice.

1940 — Dukhan I, the first successful Qatari oil well, is discovered.

1947 — Oil production begins for commercial purposes.

1949 — Export of Qatari oil begins; Sheikh Abdullah abdicates, and is followed by his son, Sheikh Ali bin Abdullah Al-Thani.

1950 — The Qatari population is about 25,000.

1952 — The first public primary school is opened. Shell Petroleum of the Netherlands is awarded a contract to search for offshore oil.

1956 — The Ministry of Education is formed.

1956-1964 — Danish archeologists identify some two hundred sites where Stone Age humans had lived some 50,000 years ago.

1963 — The Ras Abu Aboud power station begins generating electricity for Doha.

1968 — Leaders of Bahrain, Qatar, and the seven Trucial emirates meet to establish a federation; the first phase of the Umm Said Industrial District opens.

1970 — Qatar withdraws from the unification talks and decides to establish an independent state. A provisional constitution (Basic Law) provides limited constitutional forms; Qatar becomes the first Lower Gulf sheikhdom to adopt a written constitution.

1971 — Qatar decides not to join the Federation of Arab Emirates, and declares independence; it also becomes a full member of the United Nations and the Arab League. It also joins the Organization of Petroleum Exporting Countries. The huge North Field natural-gas reserve is discovered.

1972 — Sheikh Khalifah deposes Sheikh Ahmad in a bloodless coup and assumes power as the ruler of the country.

1973 — Qatar joins in the Arab oil embargo against the United States; a fertilizer plant begins production of ammonia and urea fertilizer.

1974 — Oil production is at its peak with 600,000 barrels a day.

1975 — The number of elected representatives of the *Majlis a'Shura* increases from 20 to 30 members.

1977 — Sheikh Hamad bin Khalifah Al-Thani is appointed heir apparent; the University of Qatar is established; the Ras Abu Fontas power-generating station opens; Qatar gains national control over petroleum and natural-gas resources.

1978 — Qatar's first steel mill opens.

1979 — Qatar breaks diplomatic relations with Egypt over Egypt's peace treaty with Israel.

1980 — The Qatar National Fishing Company is established to promote fishing in the surrounding waters of Qatar.

1980-88 — Qatar supports Iraq in the Iran-Iraq War.

1981 — Qatar is a founding member of the Gulf Cooperation Council (GCC) with other five nations.

1985 — The University of Qatar moves to a new campus.

1986 — The Earth Station of Satellite Communications links Qatar with the Arab world through the Arabsat satellite; dispute erupts with Bahrain over control of offshore reefs.

1987 — Diplomatic relations with Egypt are restored.

1988 — Diplomatic relations are established with China and the former Soviet Union.

1990 — Qatar denounces Iraq's invasion of Kuwait and supplies troops in Allied combat against Iraq; several Palestinians are expelled.

1991 — Phase One of the North Field Gas Operation with eight offshore platforms is completed.

1992 — Work on the Ras Laffan Industrial Complex project begins; tensions arise over the border with Saudi Arabia.

1994 — A Qatari horse is named World Champion Mare at the Paris Horse Show; Qatar boycotts a meeting of the GCC in Saudi Arabia; the Israeli Deputy Minister of Foreign Affairs makes an official visit to Qatar.

1995 — In a nonviolent palace coup, Sheikh Hamad bin Khalifah Al-Thani deposes his father as emir of Qatar.

1996 — Work continues on the development of the North Field natural gas field; Qatar has 5 percent of the world's natural gas reserves. Sheikh Jassem bin Hamad Al-Thani is named heir apparent.

IMPORTANT PEOPLE

Sheikh Abdallah bin Khalifah Al-Thani, appointed prime minister and minister of the interior in 1996.

Sheikh Abdullah bin Qasim Al-Thani, ruled Qatar from 1913 to 1949; in 1935 he signed a concession with the Iraq Petroleum Company that led to the discovery of oil in 1939.

Sheikh Ali bin Abdullah Al-Thani, emir from 1949 to 1960, he signed a concession to develop Qatar's offshore oil fields in the Persian Gulf.

Sheikh Ahmad bin Ali Al-Thani, emir from 1960 to 1972; he was the ruler of Qatar at the time of independence; he was deposed by his cousin, Sheikh Khalifah.

Sheikh Khalifah bin Hamad Al-Thani, emir from 1972 to 1995; also known as the "Father of the Nation;" a wise, pious, energetic, and powerful ruler, he led Qatar into the modern world.

Sheikh Hamad bin Abdullah Al-Thani, heir apparent and deputy ruler from 1940 to 1948; however, his untimely death in 1948 prevented him from being emir.

Sheikh Hamad bin Khalifah Al-Thani, the present ruler of Qatar, he deposed his father in June 1995; he has initiated programs to continue the modernization of Qatar and encouraged the citizens to participate in government.

Sheikh Jassem bin Hamad Al-Thani, named heir apparent in October 1966; a recent graduate of Sandhurst Military Academy.

Sheikh Muhammad bin Thani, the first ruling sheikh of Qatar; he ruled from 1850 to 1878.

Sheikh Qasim bin Muhammad Al-Thani, ruled Qatar from 1878 to 1913. He was a great warrior who constructed roads, as well as schools for religious education; he converted to the Wahhabi branch of Sunni Islam in later years.

Sheikh Rahmah ibn Jabir, one of the most notorious pirates of the nineteenth century in the gulf region.

Sheikha Mozea Al-Misnad, wife of the emir, she has been active in educational and social reform.

Compiled by Chandrika Kaul, Ph.D.

INDEX

Page numbers that appear in **boldface type** indicate illustrations

About the Authors

Byron D. Augustin is Professor of Geography and Planning at Southwest Texas State University in San Marcos , Texas. He is a Middle East specialist who serves as the executive director for the Texas committee on U.S.-Arab Relations. An award-winning teacher, he has received four Malone Fellowships, which have taken him to Qatar, Saudi Arabia, Bahrain, Oman, and the United Arab Emirates.

Dr. Augustin is a professional photographer with more than five hundred published photos. His photos have appeared in *Bahrain, Saudi Arabia, Honduras, Guatemala,* and other Enchantment of the World books. He and his wife currently have a photo exhibit, "Images of Arabia," on national tour.

Rebecca A. Augustin was graduated from Northwest Missouri State University in Maryville, Missouri, with degrees in elementary education and supervision and curriculum. She has taught at both the elementary and university level and has received the prestigious Distinguished Teaching Achievement Award from the National Council on Geographic Education and the Cram Award for Curriculum Development.

Mrs. Augustin has traveled extensively in the Persian Gulf region and received a Malone Fellowship to Saudi Arabia and Qatar. An avid photographer, her photos have appeared in both domestic and foreign publications. She and her husband frequently present teacher-education workshops on Arabic and Islamic culture.